Supplementary Volun

CW00446988

TOWARDS A 1EAT OF

'ANTHOLOGIA LATINA'

by

D. R. SHACKLETON BAILEY

THE CAMBRIDGE PHILOLOGICAL SOCIETY
1979

ISBN: 0 906014 01 8

Printed by the Cambridge University Library

ACKNOWLEDGEMENTS

During a brief visit to Lund in 1977 I was able to discuss a number of these problems with Dr Lennart Håkanson, who kindly allows me to mention several of his extempore proposals. I am also indebted to Professors C.P. Jones and E.J. Kenney and to Dr J. Diggle for some helpful comments; also to my colleague Dr Richard Thomas, whose vigilance eliminated a quantity of mechanical errors from my final typescript.

Publication in this form has been rendered possible by financial support from the Loeb Classical Library Foundation.

D. R. Shackleton Bailey
Cambridge, Mass., 1978

INTRODUCTION

Many of the pieces which make up A. Riese's part of 'Anthologia Latina' had been previously edited several times. The most important collective editions are those of J.J. Scaliger (Lyons, 1573), P. Pithoeus (Paris, 1590), P. Burman junior (Amsterdam, 1759, 1773), J.C. Wernsdorf (Altenberg, 1780-89), H. Meyer (Leipzig, 1835), A. Riese, ed. 1 (Leipzig, 1869-70), E. Baehrens (*Poet. Lat. Min.* IV (1882)), and the still ruling Teubner, A. Riese, ed. 2 (1894).

Many poems are preserved only in the uncial codex Salmasianus (A) of the seventh or early eighth century. According to Traube (*Philol.* 50 (1895) 124 = *Kl. Schr.* III 51) it is the work of a Spanish scribe: 'Seine Kenntnisse im Lateinischen waren gering, aber gerade ausreichend, ihm, der von dem Inhalt des Abzuschreibenden wenig genug verstand, allerlei geläufigere Wortbilder vorzuzaubern. Es war ein rechter Halbgebildeter und, philologisch betrachtet, ein arger Interpolator.'

Other MSS used by Riese and cited in my notes from his apparatus are:

E	=	Vossianus L. F. 111 (cod. Ausonii, s. IX)
L	=	Lipsiensis I 74 (s. IX-X)
B	=	Parisinus 8071, olim Thueaneus (s. IX-X)
S	=	Bellovacensis deperditus (aet. incertae)
V	=	Vossianus Q. 86 (s. IX)

sched. Divion. = schedae Divionenses (v. Riese, praef. xxxii ff.)

Note in addition the following with reference to particular poems:

4	P	=	cod. Prudentii antiquissimus (s. VI)
5-6	L	=	Vossianus Q. 9 (s. VI)
5-6	B	=	Vratislaviensis (s. IX)
31	S	=	Sangallensis 899 (s. IX)
388a	B	=	Berolinensis Diezianus B.66 (s. VIII-IX)
485	P	=	Parisinus 7530 (s. VIII)
485a	P	=	Parisinus 13048 (s. VIII)
485a	L	=	Vossianus Q. 33 (s. X)
485a	V	=	Veronensis 16B (s. IX)
490	P	=	Parisinus 2772 (s. X-XI)
490	R	=	Reginensis 215 (s. IX)
494b	V	=	Veronensis 16B (s. IX)
806	T	=	Toletanus caj. 101, 31 (anno 1449 scr.)

| 806 | E | = | Escorialensis g. III 6 (s. XIV) |
| 808 | H | = | Harleianus 3685 (s. XV) |

On the MSS of 286 (Symphosius' *Aenigmata*) see ad loc.

I follow Riese's numbering and, except where stated otherwise, reproduce his text. For critical incompetence it almost rivals Lehnert's *Declamationes maiores* of Ps.-Quintilian, though, unlike Lehnert, Riese was an enterprising and occasionally successful innovator. A few of the longer poems have been re-edited more recently but to little purpose. In periodicals the contributions of S. Mariotti and S. Timpanaro are the most noteworthy, but they cover only a small part of the area. A new edition is a desideratum.

NOTES

1 ('Ovidius Naso')

This piece consists of *argumenta* on the twelve Books of the *Aeneid,* each in ten hexameters, with a preface of five elegiac couplets, in which 'Ovid' proclaims his inferiority to Virgil, ending thus:

> adfirmo gravitate mea, me *carmine nullum*
> livoris *titulum* praeposuisse tibi.

crimine nullo . . . titulos Tollius

The correction was adopted by Baehrens, rightly, except that *titulos* should be *titulo*: 'It is through no sin of envy that I have placed myself in front of you in my title'. The construction *me praeposuisse* = *me me praeposuisse* is normal; cf. Kühner-Stegmann I. 701 fin. The title will originally have run something like 'Ovidii Nasonis in libros Aeneidis Vergilii epigrammata'.

XI. 10   *deinde duces* castris, *donec cessere, minantur.*

dein reduces L. Mueller   nocti cessere minanti E

In the last four lines of *Aen.* 11 night puts an end to the fighting and the combatants settle in their camps. Baehrens follows Müller in the first hemistich and the Vossianus (E) in the second, thereby almost making not only sense but the right sense. One further change is needed: 'dein reduces castris nocti cessere monenti'. Cf. Macrob. *Sat.* 3. 20. 8 'hora nos quietis admonet' and Sulp. Sev. *Dial.* 1. 27. 6 'umbra prolixior . . . monet non multum diei . . . superesse'; also Nemes. *Ecl.* 3. 67 'sparsas donec oves campo conducere in unum / nox iubet, uberibus suadens siccare fluorem / lactis' (and Virg. *Ecl.* 6. 85f.).

4
\<Contra paganos\>

43   . . . in risum quaerens quos *dederet* morti

quos dederet Haupt et Delisle: quodedere P

'Carmen vitiis prosodiacis scatet' (Riese). No doubt, but their number need not have been increased by this conjecture. Read *quos dedere,* comparing Coripp. *Ioh.* 1. 273 'nescitque miser quo flectere puppim'.

85   Leucadium fecit fundos curaret Afrorum;
       perdere Marcianum, *sibi* proconsul ut esset.

86 perderet ('*sc. fecit*') *coni. Riese*   sibi] sic vi *Baehrens*

Perhaps: 'perdere Marcianum studuit, proconsul ut esset'; cf. 51
'fundere qui incautis studuit concepta (*contrita* Haupt) venena'.

5
Precatio Terrae Matris

12   alimenta vitae tribuis perpetua fide
        et, cum *recesserit* anima, in te *refugiemus.*

13 te refugiemus *Riese*: te refugimus *LB*: tete refugimus *Baehrens*

The two 'corrections', neither of which scans, were presumably designed
to obviate the break in the resolved arsis of the third foot, -*erit a*-; cf. L.
Müller, *Res Metrica* 170. That requires another change: *recessit.* Note that
Riese perpetrates a similar metrical irregularity on his own account in line
19 of the next poem. It seems unwise to ban it here.

6
Precatio omnium herbarum

17   <praestetis etiam>, semper ut liceat mihi
        favente maiestate vestra † vos *colligere,*
        ponamque vobis fruges *et agam gratias*
        per nomen eius, qui vos iussit nascier.

19 agam gratias *Riese*: gratias agam *LB*: gratis agam *Baehrens*

Perhaps: 'vestra vos legam, / ponamque vobis fruges gratias<que>
agam'.

20 (Octavianus)

4   cum urtica <e> gremio prosilit aetherio.

e *add. Haupt*

The addition is needless, as Timpanaro has pointed out (*SCO* 10 (1961)
156 ff.). For the simple ablative with *prosilire* cf. K.-S. I.363 (add three
examples in Claudian from Birt's index). The lengthening of the vowel
before *gr* should have offended nobody (see Timpanaro).

21 (Octavianus)

A versified declamation on the following theme: 'sacrilegus capite
puniatur. de templo Neptuni aurum periit. interposito tempore piscator
piscem aureum posuit et titulo inscribsit "de tuo tibi Neptune". reus fit
sacrilegii. contra dicit. <convincitur.>'

18   prorsus magna est iniuria Nerei.
         dignus non fuerat titulis, nisi perderet aurum?
         non <*tantum*> facinus caeso est auctore piandum?
         multa patent, sed plura latent. scelus undique densum est.

         20 tantum *add. Haupt*   non facinus saevum *Baehrens*

Line 19 perhaps reads better as an exclamatory statement. The insult to
the seagod (*Nerei* = *Neptuni*) lay in the gift of his own gold, as though he
would not otherwise have been thought worthy of a dedication. Line 20 is
definitely a statement, and the missing word is not *tantum* but *unum*.

26   *sit* similis vindicta malo (nunc ipsa pudori est
         vox mea), ne magnos laedat magis ultio divos.
         audiet haec populus nosque hoc narrabimus; ergo
         quod factum est (meminisse nefas), referetur in urbe.

       26 sit *Riese*: heu *A*   29 referetur *Quicherat*: refertur *A*: referuntur *Haupt*

The gods might be hurt more by the telling of the shameful story than by
the sacrilege itself. Thus:

         heu similis vindicta malo! nunc ipsa pudori est
         vox mea, ne magnos laedat magis ultio divos.
         audiet haec populus nosque hoc narrabimus; ergo
         quod factum est meminisse nefas referetur in urbe.

'quod factum est meminisse nefas' = 'factum quod meminisse nefas est'.

42   non ager in voto est illi fortesque iuvenci,
         non inlex faenus, non classica, non pia Musa,
         sed spretis *divum* rebus placet omnibus istud:
         fraus, dolus et furtum pelagi.

       44 spretis divum *Haupt*: spretis (durŏ *superscr.*) *A*: spretis duris (*vel* rectis) *Baehrens*:
spretis dudum *Riese olim*

Read *spretis duro* (i.e. 'spretis rebus omnibus duro placet istud'). *duro* =
duri ingenii homini; cf. *Thes.* V. 1. 2309. 72.

50   illic sollicite <*per*> saxa madentia *curas*
         disponens imoque trahens animalia fundo
         serus furtivum referebat munus ad urbem.
         † *sed palam sane viderunt moenia,* saepe
         dum relevant populos vario commercia pisce.

55   cernere erat genus omne maris, conpleret ut urbem.

       50 curas] chordas *Maehly*   53 sed (set) *Riese*: nec *A*   viderunt *Petschenig*:
maduerunt *A*   54 relebat *A, corr. Petschenig*

In line 50 *curas* seems impossible, a 'psychological' error due to *sollicite*,
perhaps replacing *saetas*. In 53 *nec palam sane* translates with

palaeographical ease into *nigra iam sanie* and *maduerunt* is sound. The
comma should follow *saepe* (on *iam . . . saepe* see *Thes.* VII. 1. 115. 23).
moenia = urbs.

An editor who put two conjectures into his text and decked them with an
obelus had a peculiar conception of his duties.

95   pro *vili,* summa potestas,
            bis tibi calcato facta est iniuria caelo.

> 95 pro vili, summa *Riese (?)*: prost uilissuma *A*: pro vilis summa *Haupt*

tibi = Neptuno. Read 'pro fluctus summa potestas!' For *fluctus* 'meton.
saepe i. q. mare' see *Thes.* VI. 945. 40.

129   templum est, unde istud sublatum dicimus aurum.
            maxima res: venerandus honos, custodia nulla...

res = divitiae. The colon should be a comma.

135   ingressos *nullos servat* custodia, nulla
            egressos, licet <et> semper discurrere ad aras,
            omnibus et simulacra modis contingere *miris*.

Dr Håkanson has corrected line 135: *nulla observat*. In the next line
remove the comma after *aras* (Baehrens does not have it). Whoever wrote
137 in its present form was thinking of Virg. *Georg.* 1. 477 (from Lucr. 1.
123), but *miris* is nonsense here. Perhaps the original had *multis*.

166   scilicet horrescit, *prisco sine* nomine avorum
            ne cadat in fasces, miser undique, solus ubique!
            an non hoc genus est, cuius de examine multo
            quisquis honoratos respexit forte *potentes*
170   ob meritum fulgere viros, mox improbus, audax,
            fortunam incusans et tetro lividus ore
            pauperiem monstrat superis ac pectore laevo
            dira quiritatus fundit convitia caelo?

> 166 prisco sine *Quicherat*: priscos ne *A, Baehrens*   167 ne cadat in *Maehly*:
> incedat in *A*: incidit in *Quicherat*: incidat in *Haupt*: infamet *Baehrens*   169
> honoratus . . . parentes *A*

As often, Riese's choice of conjectures has merely spread corruption. In
166f. Baehrens understood the sense: a poor wretch like the fisherman did
not have to worry about disgracing consular ancestors by his
(dishonoured) name. But *infamet* is too far away from *incedat in. dedeceat*
would be closer, *indeceat* (see *Thes.* s.v.) closer still; cf. Val. Max. 2. 2. 3
'quod amplissimi honoris maiestatem tam taetro facinore inquinaverat'.

In 169 whoever conjectured *potentes* was misguided. The context
concerns ancestry; cf. 165 'non clarus genitor, non noto semine mater.'
parentes came from *parentis* (gen. with *meritum*).

178   an non sunt isti, quorum de nomine multi,
            ducere concessis dum nolunt artibus aevum,
180   caedibus infamant silvas et crimine cauto
            insidias tendunt domibus gregibusque rapinas?
            in quibus haut ulla est caro de sanguine cura;
            pactas *temporibus* vendunt in proelia mortes.

183 pastas A

Poor men become *either* brigands and thieves (180 f.) *or* gladiators (182 f.). Read 'aut, quibus . . . cura, / pactas' *sqq. in* will have come from *insidias* above. I make nothing of *temporibus* and substitute *corporibus*: 'nomina numina munera, corpora pectora tempora passim confunduntur' (Housman on Manil. 1. 416). Cf. 490. 14 *corpora* P, *tempora* R.

204   hoc [*sc.* auro] Mida ieiunus, Paris *ultus*

altus A

The vulgate *ultus,* whatever its provenance or supposed meaning, is a scandalous *Schlimmbesserung.* According to one version of the story (cf. E. Wust, *RE* XVIII. 4. 1491. 50), Paris was secretly handed over by his mother to the shepherd by whom he was reared (*altus*). Naturally the shepherd would be paid, so that Paris' survival makes an appropriate item in a catalogue of calamities due to gold.

209   quod ferrum intundit, *liquidus* quod conficit ignis

Fire can be called *liquidus* in the right context (cf. C. Bailey on Lucr. 6. 205), but the epithet would be merely ornamental here. Read *liquidum* (sc. *aurum*), comparing Cic. *Inv.* 1. 20 'si eum benevolum, attentum, docilem confecerit' (sc. *oratio*) *et sim.* (*Thes.* IV. 201. 3). Admittedly *conficere* can mean 'melt', as in 324. 5 *confectis* (sc. *sole*) *pinnis* (q.v.).

243   'qui raperet, totum templis non redderet.' ergo
            hoc quoque sic vincam, verum fatearis ut ipse.
            sustuleras templis; partiris, perfide, furtum;
            non totum reddis: superavit copia mentem.

245 sustulleras *A*   246 mentem] multum *Maehly*: partem *Baehrens*: votum *coni. Riese*

I proposed to read 'plus tuleras: templis partiris'. The dative (instead of *cum templis*) is then analogous to that common in later Latin with *communicare* (*Thes.* III. 1957. 14). This suggested an improvement to Dr. Håkanson: 'sustuleras tu plus. partiris'. Either way *furtum* should be followed by a comma. *mentem* is sound. The thief *had* intended to restore all the stolen gold, but there was so much of it that he changed his mind and kept some back.

23
Verba amatoris ad pictorem

Six verses. In the first four the painter is told to paint the girl in all her beauty without concealment. Then:

> te quoque pulset amor, cruatient pigmenta medullas;
> si bonus es pictor, *miseri* suspiria pinge.

The final injunction makes no sense. Suppose sighs could be painted, where would the painter's sighs (not the poet's; that would be irrelevant to the preceding line) belong in the portrait? *miseri* represents *miser in* (i.e. *miserī*). For *in suspiria pinge*, 'paint to sigh (fall in love)', cf. phrases like Ps.-Quint. *Decl. Mai.* (Lehnert) p. 196. 11 'o in lacrimas artifex nostras!' (3Thes. VII. 1. 767. 4).

24
Amans amanti

3   marcent post *rorem* violae, rosa perdit odorem

Read *florem* (cf. Colum. *R. R.* 2. 11. 10 'diebus quadraginta, quibus post florem ad maturitatem devenit'), and see below.

25
Rescriptum

> Non redit in florem, sed munus perdit amantis,
> quidquid vile iacet. dulce est, quodcumque negatur.

The first line is obscure. Perhaps the two which originally followed it have dropped out, since the reply would naturally be in the same number of verses as the invitation, i.e. six, not (as we have it) four. The present line 2 should begin 'quidquid vile (sc. *est*), iacet'.

31
De uvis

> Vindicat ipsa suos, quos pertulit, uva labores;
> quae *pede dum* premitur, subtrahit ipsa pedem.

dum premitur *AL*: cum premitur *S*: quod premitur *vulg. olim*: comprimitur *Baehrens*

For *pede dum* read *pedibus*?

35
De vipera

> Accensa in Venerem serpens genitalibus auris
> sic coit ut perimat, sic parit ut pereat.
> hi sunt affectus, haec oscula digna venenis,
> †coniugioque Venus semper amore nocens.

1 arvis *Hagen (cf. Virg. Georg. 3. 136)*   3 digna] tincta *Wakefield*   4
coniugiique *Baehrens*: coniungitque *coni. Riese*

Does *auris* echo *genitabilis aura Favoni?*
There is nothing amiss with the second couplet. *digna venenis* means
'worthy of poisonous creatures;' cf. 99. 4 'hinc lacerasse ferunt saeva
venena virum'. The pentameter means: *et haec Venus digna venenis est,
amore semper coniugio* (i.e. *coniugibus) nocens*. The fable that sexual
intercourse between snakes has fatal results for both participants goes
back to Herodotus (3. 109).

58
De Aegypto et Danao

Perfida nox Danai dirarum caede sororum;
    mitis *Hypermestrae* perfida nox Danai.

2 mitis sipermestrę perfidę *A*

Read 'mitis Hypermestre, perfida' *sqq.*; cf. Prop. 4. 7. 67 'narrat
Hypermestre magnum ausas esse sorores' (same form in 63; Ovid (*Her*. 14.
1) has the nominative *Hypermestrā*).

60
De Calypso et Didone

Inputat aegra toris *vim per* deserta Calypso;
    vim Dido incensis inputat aegra toris.

1 vim (*Oudendorp*) per *Riese*: qui pfert *A*: quia (*vel* quod) flet *Baehrens*   2
incensis *Baehrens*: inpensis *A*: infensis *D'Orville*

For *qui pfert* read *quae fert*, 'her sufferings'? The pentameter means that
Dido blames her own (self-directed) violence on the bed to which she has
set fire.

64
De Procne et Philomela

Sanguine muta probat facinus Philomela sorori,
    vimque vice linguae sanguine muta probat.

1 sanguine] stamine *Maehly*   2 et vice vim *D'Orville*: inque vicem *Maehly*: vim
querulae *Baehrens*   sanguine] stamine *Maehly*

D'Orville's is the best answer in the first half of the pentameter, since
inque vicem leaves *probat* without an object. *stamine* is misconceived.
Philomela is supposed to have used her blood to represent what had
happened; cf. 27.3 'sanguis inest pingitque cruor tormenta pudoris.'

83
\<Epistula. Dido Aeneae\>

The poem is in the manner of the pseudo-Quintilianic Longer Declamations, full of strained and obscure conceits, lacking overall coherence. But it is not the nonsense which copyists and editors between them have made of it.

18   a, quotiens revocata manus, *dubiumque* pependit!
      quid factura fuit trepidanti pollice!

      18 dubitansque *Maehly*

The exclamation-mark after *pependit,* an aberration of modern editors, should disappear, making 'quid . . . pollice' an indirect question (the indicative *fuit* is unremarkable in a late author). Maehly's correction of *dubiumque* may be right; cf. Luc. 5. 602 'dubium pendet, vento cui concidat, aequor'.

22   torsit iter male tractus apex dubiaque remissus
      mente pudor, dum verba notat, dum nomina mandat
      flamma nocens, *iram tardans*; penitusque cucurrit
      sopitus per membra calor diroque medullas
      igne vorat.

    24 iram (*Hoeufft*) tardans *Riese*: irata redens *A*: irata ardens *Birt*: iterata redit *Petschenig,* alii alia

This had better become:

      torsit iter male tractus apex, dubiaque remissus
      mente pudor dum verba notat, dum nomina mandat,
      flamma nocens iterata redit

'remissus pudor dum verba notat' = 'remisso pudore dum verba notat Dido'.

31   meus ista meretur
      affectus? non ille torus, non conscia lecti
      sacramenta tenent? totum *pro* crimine perdo,
      quidquid amore dedi.

    33 perdo *Higtius*: perdi *A*   totum, pro, crimine perdo *Baehrens*

Read: 'totum quo crimine perdo / quidquid amore dedi?' Cf. Stat. *Silv.* 5. 4. 1 'crimine quo merui . . . ?'

36   sed regna petebas
      debita, nec *mecum* poteras coniungere *sortem*?

37 mecum . . . coniungere *Riese*: rerum . . . conuincere *A*: rerum . . . convertere *Baehrens*

Not a question, but a plea advanced on Aeneas' behalf (so earlier editors). Read 'rerum . . . pervincere'; cf. 118. 3 'fas nulli est humanam vincere sortem'.

38   si datur ire, placet. nam quod fugis, unde *recursus,*
        vota "nocentis' habes; nihil est, quod *dura* querellis
40   verba fidemque voco; quisquis mea vulnera deflet,
        invidiam fecisse neget. trahit omnia casus.
        dum sortem natura *rapit,* 'sua taedia solus
        fallere nescit amor'.

42 sorte *A*   rapit] capit *Petschenig:* parit *Baehrens*

'si datur ire, placet' means: 'if it is *allowable* (let alone necessary) for you to leave, I approve.' She can say that, for (*nam*) clearly it is *not* allowable. It would be a sin against gratitude, and Aeneas' prayers (for a safe voyage) would be the prayers of a guilty man (and would get the answer they deserved); cf. 98 'tantum quis in hospite vellet / hoc audere nefas? quis vota nocentis habere?' But 'unde recursus' invites hariolation such as Riese's: 'quod ad me redire poteris, ego "nocens" votis meis te ire iubeo'. The copyist may have understood his *recursus* in the late (?)-mediaeval sense of *refugium* (see Du Cange, s.v. 4). Read: 'nam quod fugis unde receptus, / vota nocentis habes'. 'unde receptus' = 'eam a qua receptus es'; cf. K.-S. II. 284 f. In the next sentence *dura* cannot qualify *verba*; the reference must be to Aeneas' delusive promises. Read *vana* (*quoduana / quoduna / quod dura*). A comma should follow *casus* in 41, then: 'non' (or 'nec') 'sortem' (i.e. *fatum*) 'natura capit'. The refrain 'sua taedia solus / fallere nescit amor' begins a new section of the poem.

54   iam Philomela tacet damno male *victa* pudoris

victa *Burman:* picta *A*

I had thought of *damno mulcata.* But may not *picta* refer to the cloth on which Philomela painted what had happened? See on poem 64 above.

68   fessus iuga solvit arator
        et noctem per vota capit: reparare labores
70   novit grata quies, nec cessat reddere vires
        infusus per membra sopor *rurisque* ministram
        ruricolis dat semper opem.

71 rurisque] noctisque *vulg. olim:* lucisque *Baehrens*

Read *durisque*; cf. Virg. *Georg.* 1. 160 'duris agrestibus' (sim. *Aen.* 7. 504).

87   vota *queror:* vellem *tacitis* peritura querellis
        flere domo, vellem <*iam*> *tabida fundere* fletus.
        sed negat ipse dolor, quod iam pudor ante negavit;
        scribere iussit amor miseram me, cuius honestam
        fecit culpa fidem.

87 nota *vulg. olim*   88 iam tabida fundere *Riese* (*!*): tacitus (o *super* u *scr.*)
umere fletus *A*: tacitos consumere fletus *Burman*

vota queror and *nota queror* are impossible, but I suspect the fault lies
with the verb, a stopgap supplied from *querellis* to replace the loss of
quidem. Read *tectis* for *tacitis,* because Burman's easy correction in the
next line should be accepted, as it was by Baehrens. Repunctuation will do
the rest:

> vota quidem vellem tectis peritura querellis
> flere domo, vellem tacitos consumere fletus,
> sed negat ipse dolor. quod iam pudor ante negavit,
> scribere iussit amor. miseram me, cuius honestam
> fecit culpa fidem! poteram dispergere ponto
> membra *sqq.*

'miseram me' starts a new *motif*: it was only Dido's love (*culpa*) which
had prevented her from destroying Aeneas and his son in violation of the
laws of hospitality (*fidem*).

96   sed nostro pectore pulsum
> cessit amore nefas et honesta pericula *passus*
> corda ligavit amor.

97 cessit *Schrader*: crescit *A*

Read *passi.* Like Desdemona, Dido loved her hero for the dangers he
had passed; cf. 136 'tutior esse times et honesta pericula poscis'.

98   *quis tantum* in hospite vellet
> hoc audere nefas? quis vota nocentis habere?
> nullus amor sub †laude latet.

100 laude *A*: corde *sched. Divion.*: labe *Baehrens*: fraude *coni. Riese*

Metri causa perhaps read *tantum quis.* This poem contains two elisions,
both with *-que,* and no hiatus; though *vel* counts as long before *hoc* in 119,
if sound (see ad loc.).

Dido spared Aeneas because she loved him. 'tantum quis . . . habere?' is
an imagined objection: nobody would have wished to incur the guilt of
such a crime, love or no love. Dido's rejoinder is not immediately easy to
follow, but I think *laude* is sound: 'love never hides behind men's praise'.
She had not spared Aeneas because she wanted to gain credit for being a
good hostess (or to escape blame for being a bad one); lovers do not
pretend that they do what they do, or do not do what they do not do, out of
regard for praise or blame; they acknowledge their real motive, love.

106   dulcis mea colla fovebat
> Ascanius miserumque puer figebat amorem,
> cui modo nostra fides amissam reddere matrem

dum cupit, *hoc* verum mentito pignore nomen
format amor

107 figebat Oudendorp: fouebat A

ut (= *velut*) for *hoc* in 109 would make matters easier. Dido wants to be a mother to Ascanius in place of the one he has lost. Her love for Aeneas 'fashions the name' (of mother) as though it were true, whereas in literal fact it was only in pretence that she called Ascanius her child (*mentito pignore*) or herself his mother.

117   nihil est, quod dura reposcam:
nequiquam donasse velim! quae perdere possem,
numquam damna voco. vel hoc mihi, perfide, redde,
quod sibi debet amor, si nil pia facta merentur.
esse deos natura docet; non esse timendos,
rerum facta probant.

118 nequiquam *Riese*: nec quidquid *A*: nec quidquam *Burman*: hoc quidquid *Baehrens2*   119 voco⁺ volo *vulg. olim*

Read: 'nihil est quod dura reposcam / quidquid nec donasse velim'. She means: 'Don't suppose I shall be so unkind as to ask you to give back anything which I could wish I had not bestowed in the first place', i.e. material benefits as opposed to love (she could not regret her gift of love, having had no choice in the matter). 'I don't call things which I might have lost anyway "losses"' (Riese has a strange note: '*voco*, i.e. in eum advoco'). 'The only payment I ask is what love owes itself (i.e. love in return for love)'. *vel* apparently = *saltem*, a post-classical use. *sed* would be easier (see on 98 above), or *solum*.

What follows only needs a rational punctuation: '. . . amor. si nil pia facta merentur, / esse deos natura docet, non esse timendos / rerum facta probant'. If good deeds go unrewarded, then, while nature teaches us that the gods exist, the facts of life show that they have no power.

124   improbe dure nocens crudelis perfide fallax
officiis ingrate meis! quid verba minantur?
non odit, qui vota dolet, nec digna rependit,
quidquid † *lexa* gemit.

126 digna] dicta *Baehrens*   127 laesa *vulg. olim*: plexa *Heinsius*: rixa *Baehrens*

After the string of abusive epithets Dido asks: 'What threat is there in words?' 'non odit qui vota dolet' I take to mean: one who grieves at his prayers, i.e. grieves as he prays for vengeance or at the thought of his prayers taking effect, does not really hate. In line 127 *laesa* should be restored (what is *plexa*?): 'an injured woman's *groans* do not requite the wrongdoer as he deserves.' But I have little doubt that *quisquis* (fem.)

should replace *quidquid*: an injured woman who grieves does not (i.e. would not if she could) inflict condign punishment. Either way it is a question whether *quae* should not replace *qui* in 126; and the comma after *rependit* should be removed. The coincidence with the refrain in this part of the poem ('cui digna rependes, / si mihi dura paras?') seems to be unintentional.

127   tibi nempe remissus habetur
       lege pudoris amor! *qui* tanta dedisse recusem:
       sceptra domum Tyrios regnum Carthaginis arces
130   et quidquid regnantis erat? de coniuge, fallax,
       non de iure queror, meritum si non habet ardor:
       sed quod hospes eras, *nec* te magis esse nocentem
       quam miserum, Troiane, puto, qui digna repellis,
       dum non digna cupis.

   127 nempe *Baehrens*: me pe *A*   128 qui (= quomodo) *Riese*: cui
   A   134 dum *Oudendorp*: sum *A*

Reading with earlier editors *amor, cui* and returning the question into a statement, I take Dido to mean: 'I suppose you think the law of shame allows you to give up loving me because I (as you imagine) regret giving you all those items' (*dedisse recusem = dedisse nollem*): i.e. 'you are ashamed that I have given you so much and now want to take it back, and so you think you are no longer obliged to love me' – such shame being basically incompatible with love.

   She answers: 'de coniuge, fallax, / non de iure queror. meritum si non habet ardor, / sed quod hospes eras, non te' *sqq.* 'I am not complaining of you as a debtor but as a husband. If it is not my love but my hospitality that puts you in my debt (i.e. if it is a matter of material benefits), I think you are as much to be pitied for your folly as blamed for your ingratitude. For you are throwing away those very benefits.'

148   licet simul improbus exul
       et malus hospes eras et ubique timendus *haberis*:
       vive tamen nostrumque nefas post fata memento!

   149 malus *Baehrens*: maius *A*   haberis] ameris *Oudendorp*

Aeneas was still in Carthage, and the report of his infidelity could not have already travelled around the world. For *haberis* read *abibis*. 'nostrumque nefas' = 'the wrong you have done me'.

93
De iudicio Salomonis
Inventa est ferro pietas prolemque *necando*

conservat mater, contemto pignore victrix.

1 necando vulg.: negando A

In Housman's phrase, the author pays for the ignorance and sloth of editors. In III Kings 3 the true mother saves the child's life by abandoning it to the false one, i.e. by disclaiming it (*negando*). I take *pignore* as 'the stake' rather than as = *filio*.

100

De templo Veneris quod ad muros <extruendos dirutum est>

3   nam *qua delectis* volvuntur saxa *catervis*
         hac sunt murorum mox relocanda minis.

3 qua] quae Oudendorp   delectis ('an conductis?') Riese: deiectis A: detectis Maehly   catervis] cavernis Maehly   4 hac Meyer: haec A

Read: 'nam quae deiectis v. s. columnis, / haec' *sqq.*

101

De basterna

5   provisum est caute, ne per loca publica pergens
         fucetur visis casta marita viris.

6 fucetur Salmasius: fugetur A: fuscetur B

fucetur is right, but does not mean 'blush', as generally supposed. For *fucare* = *vitiare, corrumpere* in late Latin see *Thes.* VI. 1459. 84.

103

De homine qui per se molebat

7   per te namque terens Cererem patiere labores,
         quos quaerens natam *pertulit* ipsa Ceres.

If this is right, *quos* has to be understood as *quantos*. But *non* (or *nec*) *tulit* would be preferable.

112

De funambulo

Stuppea suppositis tenduntur vincula lignis,
    quae fido ascendit docta iuventa gradu.
quae super aërius protendit crura viator
    vixque avibus facili tramite currit homo.

2 quae vulg.: quem ABV   3 quae vulg.: quam ABV: iam Baehrens

quae can hardly be right in both places. In line 3 perhaps read *cum* (*quom*) for *quam*, with comma after *gradu.*

113
De citharoedo

5   nam sic aequali ambo (*sc.* bracchia et linguam) moderamine
librat
    atque oris socias temperat arte manus,
    ut dubium tibi sit gemina dulcedine capto,
    vox *utrumne* canat an lyra sola sonet.

5 nam sic *Riese*: namq; ita *A*: nam lira *B*   8 utrumne *Pithoeus*: utrumque *A*:
atrum *B*

Voice and instrument are so blended into one that the sound seems to
come from a single source, whether that be the voice or the instrument.
Read *tantumne* (= *utrum tantum modo*).

114
Aliter

9   ars laudanda nimis, cuius moderamine *sacro*
    unum ex diversis vox digitique canunt!

For *sacro* perhaps read *docto* or *certo,* or as Dr Håkanson suggests,
vafro.

116
Laus temporum quattuor

3   indicat autumnum redimito palmite vertex.
    frigore pallet hiems designans *alite* tempus.

4 alite *AV*: ali *B*

Winter marks the end of the year – with its wing? *alite* seems to come
from *(p)almite* above. The right word will be *limite,* often used of time-
division; cf. *Thes.* VII. 2. 1416. 9, especially Mar. Victor, *Aleth.* 1. 109
'signataque limite certo / tempora dissiciens' (sc. *sol*). *limite signare* of
boundaries is Virgilian and Ovidian.

117
Laus omnium mensium

13   Quintilis *mensis* Cereali germine *gaudet*;
    Iulius a magno Caesare nomen habet.

13 messis *Heinsius*

mensis, clearly an interpolation, replaced *quondam* (*qđ*?), which can ill be
spared, and brought another corruption in its train, *gaudet* for *gaudens*
(remove the semicolon). 'Quintilis quondam' = mensis qui quondam
Quintilis erat.'

124
De thermis

Delectat variis infundere corpora lymphis
et mutare *maris* saepe fluenta libet.
nam ne consuetae pariant fastidia thermae,
hinc iuvat alterno tingere membra lacu.

2 et . . . maris *Meyer*: ut . . . magis *A*: vel . . . maris *Baehrens*

The sea has no business here. Read: *et . . . vagis.* The bathers kept moving
from one pool to the other.

126
<De bibliotheca in triclinium mutata>

Tecta novem *Phoebi nuper* dicata Camenis
nunc retinet Bacchus et sua *tecta* vocat.

1 Phoebo (foebo *man. rec. in A*) nuperque *Heinsius*   dicata] dictata *Baehrens*:
devota *Sedlmayer*

The standard of versification in the group to which this epigram belongs
warrants correction of *dīcata.* Heinsius' is much the best. It also warrants
replacement of *tecta* (repeated from line 1) by *templa* in line 2. Cf. Mart. 12.
3(2). 7 'iure tuo veneranda novi pete limina templi, / reddita Pierio sunt ubi
tecta' (Heinsius, *templa* codd.) 'choro'. The two words are often confused;
see Friedländer ad loc.

128
Ad lenonem comitiacum

7   effuge vitandos, si qua potes arte, labores
      ut valeas tenso vivere, leno, pede.

8 valeas *Salmasius*: caleas *A*: careas *Petschenig*: caveas *Bolt*

A pimp who wants to become an army officer is advised against it.
Line 8 makes no sense in the vulgate. The word to correct is not *caleas*
but *ut*: 'cur caleas tenso vivere, leno, pede?' 'Why should you be eager to
live at full stretch?' (i.e. to exchange the soft life of a pimp for the strenuous
life of a soldier). For *tenso pede* = (πάντα) κάλων ἐκτείνων cf. Otto, *Röm.
Sprichwörter* s.v. *velum* (363). *calere = vehementer cupere* is found in Statius
and Claudian; see *Thes.* III. 148. 71.

130
De Caballina meretrice

5   hirsutis tamen est petenda mulis,
      qui possint pariles citare *iunctas.*

Caballina had a lovely complexion, but also a disagreeable habit of kicking like a mule. I do not know whether 'qui (*sic*) *AB*' in Riese's apparatus to line 6 merely indicates bewilderment. Certainly the line is nonsense as it stands. *pugnas* for *iunctas* will make it into sense.

131
De Arzucitano vate

8   solus ligna dolans fortibus asceis
       et duri resecans robora pectoris
       vatem te poterat reddere ligneum

9 duri *Heinsius*: duris *A*

et cannot be connective. I had proposed *tam duri* or *praeduri*, but *haec duri* (Håkanson) may be right. In any case we are to understand that it would take a more than usually expert carpenter to make such a block of wood into a poet.

132
De capone phasianacio

5   flammea sic rutilum *distinguit* pinna colorem,
       ut vibrare putes plumea membra faces.

flammea and *rutilum* seem to mean the same colour; cf. Avien. *Arat.* 81 'rutilo flagrat coma flammea crine'. How can red plumage *distinguish* red colour? The right verb may be *distendit* (= *dilatat*), though *diffundit* or *dispergit* were rather to be expected.

149
Aliter (i.e. de equa Filagri advocati. Insultatio pro concubitu)

7   fessae cornipedis fricas *hiatum*

hiatum *Baehrens*: meatum *A*

The change is completely needless; see *Thes.* VIII. 515. 35.

12   horrendum vitium est in advocato,
       orando *solitum* movere caulas
       subantis pecoris *tenere* gambas.

solitum *vulg.*: sonitum *A*

gambas is generally supposed, as in the *Thesaurus,* to be used loosely for *crura.* Properly *gamba* is the juncture of the tibia with the hoof in a horse's hind legs; here, in effect, 'hooves'. Remove the comma from line 12 and continue: 'orando solito movere caulas / subantis pecoris timere gambas'. This barrister, whose pleading moved courtrooms ('caulas' = 'cancellos tribunales'), had to fear a well-directed kick from the molested animal.

151
De Galatea

5   ipsa Cupidineae *laedunt tormenta* pharetrae,
        cuius et in mediis flamma suburit aquis.

5 laedunt *Riese*: cedunt *A*   tormenta *Baehrens*: tẹlementae *A*: elementa *vulg. olim*

Galatea is so much in love that she does not feel the pain of the thorn in her foot. Cupid's fire burns even in the depth of the sea. Of course *cedunt elementa* is right.

152
Aliter. De Galatea in vase

Fulget et in patinis ludens pulcherrima Nais,
    prandentum inflammans *ora* decore suo.
congrua non tardus *diffundat* iura minister,
    ut lateat positis tecta libido cibis.

2 ora] corda *Baehrens*   3 diffundat *vulg.*: difundat *A*

corda, not mentioned by Riese, should replace the grotesque *ora.* In line 3 read *defundat,* and for *congrua* ('appropriate' to what?) read *pinguia*; cf. Scrib. Larg. 189 'ius pingue agninum', 200 'album ius pingue et salsum'. *libido* in line 4 must be the exciting picture on the dish; cf. *libidinosus,* 'i.q. libidinem, sc. in rebus veneriis, efficiens', of which the *Thesaurus* supplies a single example, *Priap.* 47. 6 'libidinosis incitatus erucis'.

154
Aliter

3   si prandere cupis, díffer spectare figuram,
        ne tibi *ieiuno lumina tentet* amor.

4 ieiuno *Maehly*: ieiunus *A*   inguina *Maehly*   tentet *Burman*: tendat *A*

I would read 'ne tibi ieiunus inguina tendat amor'. Both *ieiunus* (cf. 126. 2 above) and *ieiuno* (cf. 135. 2, 169. 2, 197. 3) are acceptable metrically.

155
De Scaevola

3   miratur Porsenna virum poenamque relaxans
        maxima cum obsessis foedera victor init.

4 cum obsessis *corr. ex* possessis *V*

What are *maxima foedera*? Read *mutua*; cf. Claud. *Epith.* 66 'nutant ad mutua palmae / foedera'.

162
De Troia

Desine, Troia, tuos *animo* deflere labores:
Romam capta creas; merito tua postuma regnat.

The fatuous *animo* must be replaced. I prefer *tandem* to *nimium.*

173
De Marsya

1   Aërio victus dependet Marsya ramo
        nativusque probat pectora tensa rubor.
     docta manus varios lapidem limavit in *artus*;
        arboris atque hominis fulget ab arte fides.

2 tonsa Hagen   3 varios] vivos *Baehrens*   4 fides *Cannegieter*: figis *A*

The natural red of the stone suited the flayed body. *tensa* may stand; the chest was stretched by the weight of the pendent victim. *probat* means 'portray convincingly'; cf. 111. 6 (de pantomimo) 'quae resonat cantor, motibus ipse probat'. In line 3 *varios,* which leads up to the pentameter, cannot well be wrong. Perhaps *artus* should be *actus.* The stone is made to 'act out' both the tree and the man (satyr).

176
De ansere, qui intra se capit copiam prandii

5   fulcit utrumque latus turdus cum turture pinguis
        † *multaque perniferum corpore pandit* opus.

6 pulpaque *Baehrens*: vulvaque *coni. Riese*   penniferum *vulg. olim*

The different parts of the goose's body are stuffed with 'various riches of the table' (2 'varias mensae turgidus ambit opes'), including other birds; and the 'winged structure' (cf. 17 'maiorem in parvo haec monstrat fabrica technam') 'spreads out many bodies (inside itself)'. So read: 'multaque penniferum corpora pandit opus' – except that *pandit* should probably be *condit* (cf. 227. 2 below (on 228)).

179
Aliter (i.e. de balneis cuiusdam pauperis)

1   Parvula succinctis ornavit iugera Bais
        urbanos callens fundere Vita *locos.*

2 urbanos *Heinsius*: urbanus *A*   locus *A (corr. m. l)*

Read *iocos.* The pentameter merely describes Vita as a witty fellow; cf. Quint. *Inst.* 2. 5. 8 'in iocis urbanitas', Liv. 7. 2. 5 'iocularia fundentes versibus'.

190
De Bumbulo

Nominis et formae pariter ludibria gestans
 conventus nostros, Bumbule parvus, adis.
sed ratio est: *extas* longis Pygmaeus in armis,
 ne te deprensum grus peregrina voret.
5 nec frustra ostendis proprio placuisse parenti,
 quod turpis nomen sumpseris heniochi.
ille *habuit* doctas *circi prostrare* puellas;
 te duce lascivae nocte fricantur anus.

  3 extas *Riese*: mixtus *A*   7 aluit . . . circo *Burman* prostare *vulg.*

Bumbulus, then, is a midget, who has been adopted by a charioteer of evil repute and claims that this was done in conformity with the wishes of his natural father ('proprio placuisse parenti'), now deceased (see 191 below). And certainly Bumbulus is a chip off the old block, a pimp like his father, though in a somewhat different style.

In line 3 read 'sed ratio est si stas'. *armis = mentula*: see *Thes.* II. 601. 58 and cf. *hasta.* In line 7 *circo* seems necessary and *aluit* (cf. 286. XCII and Diggle on Auson. *Mos.* 306 in *Proc. Cam. Phil. Soc.* 22 (1976). 54f.) not improbable. On *prostrare,* supposedly = *prosternere* (!), Riese refers to Thielman's lucubrations in *Arch. f. lat. Lex.* 2. 63 (or rather 62 f.), but not to Juv. 3. 65 'ad circum iussas prostrare puellas'.

191
Aliter

Dum sis patris heres teneas et, Bumbule, censum
utile nec tibi sit, pietas si *laesa* probetur,
 das operam proprio auctori adversus haberi.
discordat multum contra suscepta voluntas;
5 dilexit genitor prasinum, te russeus intrat.

   3 adversus] hau diversus *Baehrens*

Baehrens was looking the wrong way. Now that Bumbulus had come into his father's money, he had no reason to maintain a reputation for *pietas.* Read *si illaesa* in line 2.

195
De elephanto

Horrida cornuto procedit belua rostro,
 quem dives nostris India misit *oris.*

I cannot believe in *ŏris.* Burman's forgotten *agris* seems the most likely substitute; cf. Sil. 9. 185 'Herculeis iter a metis ad Iapygis agros', Dracont.

Orest. 75 'cur, pater, Hectoreos peteretis classibus agros?', Avien. *Orb. terr.* 565 'Graios adiacet agros'. Cf. also Ennod. *Carm.* 2. 133. 3 'frangunt Marmaricis elephas quod misit ab arvis'.

196
Aliter

3   sed vario fugienda malo cum belua gliscat,
      est tamen *expertis* mors pretiosa feri.

4 expertis *Burman senior*: ex certis *ABV*

The death of the elephant is valuable to those who have tried it! That is how this facile conjecture is most naturally understood, though Burman junior and Gronovius took *pretiosa* as 'costly' (to the hunters). But read *excepti. excipere* is 'a regular hunting term for lying in wait for an animal, or attacking it when it comes, or both (see *Thes.* V. 2. 1254. 79-82, 1255. 2. 32-4) . . . Hence also "catch or kill in a trap", as in Virg. *Ecl.* 3. 18, Val. Flac. 6. 422' (*Propertiana* 100).

197
De circensibus

3   nam duodenigenas ostendunt ostia menses
      quaeque *ineat* cursim aureus astra iubar.

4 ineat *Riese*: meat *B*: mea *A*

For transitive *meare* see *Thes.* s.v. and Hor. *Sat.* 1. 6. 94 'aevum remeare peractum'. An indicative is preferable to a subjunctive here.

14   et medius *centri* summus obliscus *adest.*

adest *Riese*: adit *AB*: agit *Baehrens*

Read: 'centrum . . . obit'. For *obire,* 'de rebus circumstantibus, cingentibus, tegentibus *sim.*', see *Thes.* IX. 2. 48. 38.

198
Verba Achillis in parthenone cum tubam Diomedis audisset

    Vana *velut* cautae surgens formido parenti
    femineos iuvenem iussit me sumere cultus

1 cautae] captae *Baehrens*

The trouble will lie with the functionless *velut* rather than the highly relevant *cautae.* Read *nimis cautae*?

20   stamina linquentes *currant* ad spicula palmae

currant ad] curent iam *Maehly*: versanto *coni. Baehrens*

Could *currant* refer to the rapid movement of the hand in weaving? Cf. Venant. Fort. 2. 9. 6 'en stupidis digitis stimulatis tangere cordas, / cum mihi non solito currat in arte manus!'

55   sed *Danais comes esse* placet sociumque pericli
       pro famae titulis meliori adiungere causae.

55 comes esse] comitem esse *Burman*: me adesse *Baehrens* ('*poetam ipsum emendans' Riese*)

Perhaps *Danaos comitasse.* If there were a pronoun it would be *te,* not *me,* since these two lines are part of the 'coward counsellor's' (*iners monitor*) speech, which begins at 44 ('sed mihi quis referat') and ends at 58.

74   mihi iam lux amplior illa est,
       quae virtute *cluit,* quae nescit claustra sepulcri.

75 cluit *Higtius*: fluet (i *supra* e) *A*

lux = vita. 'The life which flows on (*fluit*) through valour' is the immortality of glory. For *fluere* of passing time see *Thes.* VI. 974. 2.

83   ferre potest, quaecumque †labans successibus aetas
       exigit

inhians *Baehrens*: valens *coni. Riese*

labans = deficiens is probably sound. The hero's youth will spend itself in a series of victories. *aetas, successibus labans, ferre potest quaecumque exigit* (sc. *aetas ipsa*).

199 (Vespa)
Iudicium coci et pistoris iudice Vulcano

19   sis memor, o Saturne, tuis quod praesto diebus,
       et me *prae* studio trepidum tu numine firma.

20 pro *Baehrens*

pro is right. *pro studio trepidum* means nervous on behalf of my calling (baking)'; cf. 59 'ora niger studio'.

30   provocor ut dicam: *mihi panem tu, coce,* temptas,
       quem docuit notus Cerealis fingere panes
       urbe Placentinus, cunctas qui tradidit artes.
       Pythagoras populo nescis quae suaserit olim?
       mandere ne vellent mixto cum sanguine carnes.

30 mihi panem tu, coce *Riese*: militonem tu roso *AB*: militonem tu Thraso *Wernsdorf*: mihi panem rodere *E. Abel*

'A locus desperatus. The conjectures are innumerable' (R.T. Clark, *CR* 29 (1915) 48). Despair was premature. First, the usual view (contested by Clark) that Cerealis is the name of the Baker's teacher (not = *cereales*) is

correct. This teacher appropriately came from Placentia; cf. Plaut. *Capt.*
162 'opu' Panicis est, opu' Placentinisque'. The next thing to look for is the
Baker's own name, and the place to find it is the corrupt half of line 30. And
since honey is an ingredient of *placentae* (Cato, *R. R.* 76. 3; cf. 63 'qui
tantum de melle et polline fingit / has quas iactat opes' and 73 below 'nec si
sit melleus ipse'), no name could be more fitting than 'Melito', actually
found as a cognomen in Dessau, *Inscr. Lat.* 7804 (L. Vibi Melitonis f.),
though not in Kajanto's *Latin cognomina* (also as a female name; cf. J.
Jackson, *Marginalia scaenica,* 122 f.). Read 'Melitonem rodere temptas, /
quem docuit' *sqq.* as an indignant statement or question, ending at
Placentinus. What follows, as Wernsdorf saw, concerns Pythagoras, of
whom Ovid says (*Met.* 15. 65) 'cumque animo et vigili perspexerat omnia
cura, / in medium discenda dabat'.

71   certe quem extollit, quem laudat saepius ille,
          ille *tuus* panis sine nobis, crede, placere
          solus non poterit, nec si sit melleus ipse.

  ipse is the Baker. Read *ille suus* (cf. K.-S. I 602).

87   cervinam Actaeon tollit, Meleager aprinam,
          agninam Pelias, taurinam *lingulus* Aiax.

             88 limulus *coni. Riese*

  The hapax legomenon *lingulus* is supposed to mean 'talkative' or
'quarrelsome', which Ajax emphatically was not, despite the fantasies of
early commentators; cf. H.J. Rose's characterization in the *Oxford
Classical Dictionary*: 'A blunt, stolid man, slow of speech, of unshakable
courage'. Read *longulus.* Tall (πελώριος) Ajax carried a shield like a tower
(*Il.* 7. 219). For the word, see below on 286. XXVI.

200
Pervigilium Veneris

59   cras erit, cum primus Aether copulavit nuptias.
          ut pater *totum* crearet vernis annum nubibus,
          in sinum maritus imber fluxit almae coniugis.

  60 totum *Salmasius:* totis *AB:* Iovis *Maehly*   uernis *AB:* veris *Sanadon:* vernus
Pithoeus, metri causa

  Perhaps 'ruptis crearet veris'. Cf. below on 494b. 66.

205
De castellano

10   qua *te* cumque moves, os culum porrigis ultro;
          nam *turpe est* fetore gravi, si forte loquaris;

si taceas, *fissis* secessum naribus *efflas.*

11 turpe est *Riese*: turpes *A*: torpes *B*   12 fissis *Riese*: bissis *A*: iussis *B*: binis
vulg. olim: bifidis *Baehrens*

This should go (cf. *Anth. Pal.* 11. 241, 242):

> qua tu cumque moves os, culum porrigis ultro.
> nam pedis fetore gravi, si forte loquaris;
> si taceas, vissis secessum naribus efflans.

On the verb *vis(s)io* = βδέω (not in Lewis and Short) see
Walde-Hofmann, *Lat. etym. lex.* s.v. This seems to be the only certain
example outside glossaries, but it is implied in Cic. *Fam.* 9. 22. 4 (see my
note ad. loc.). For the metre of line 10 see Housman on Manil. 3. 597. The
corruption of *pēdis* into *turpes*, due to the copyist's misunderstanding of
the former, may have been facilitated by *tu* just above.

207
De Crescituro

> Cresciture, ferox ne quid tibi dorsa flagellis
> conscindat coniunx, *iunctis* tu *pedibus* astas.

2 vinctis *Petschenig*

pedibus makes no better sense than metre. Read *postibus*? *iunctis postibus
astas* might perhaps mean 'you stand at the closed door (to protect your
back)' (cf. Luc. 5.531 'poste recluso'), but this lacks point. So perhaps read
unctis tu postibus; cf. Lucr. 4. 1179, where the *exclusus amator* covers his
mistress' threshold with flowers, 'postisque superbos / unguit amaracino
et foribus miser oscula figit' (cf. Pers. 5. 165). Here it would be the husband
who anoints the doorposts to placate a fierce wife and then uses them for
cover.

208
De Tautano

> Tautane, *infamem* nulla *quem* coniuge captum
> spiritus inmundus subito praecordia torsit,
> vendere mancipium pulcrum commune theatro

> . . . .

1 Tautane *vulg.*: Tautano *A*   *post v. 3 lacunam statuit Riese*

Read:

> Tautane, informi nulla qui coniuge captum
> spiritus inmundus subito praecordia torsit
> vendere mancipium pulcrum commune theatro?

'What unclean spirit suddenly twisted your heart to make you sell a beautiful slave to the theatre as public property, though you were not in the grip of an ugly wife?' If Tautanus *had* been married to such a wife, her jealousy might have forced him to get rid of the boy. Since he was not, his action could only be ascribed to demonic possession. The piece seems to be complete as it stands.

209

De Abcare servo dominico

Regius est Abcar servus, †*palus hispidus ursus*
rana nanus strobilus palmus zeloceca cylindrus.

palus may be for *pilus. hispidus ursus* remains baffling.

211 (Felix)

Aliter (i.e. de thermis Alianarum)

3   hoc uno rex fecit opus Thrasamundus in anno,
          inclita dans *populis* munera temporibus.

3 hoc uno *Voss*: hic unus *A*   4 parvis *vel* paucis *Oudendorp*: propriis *Baehrens*: populi *Ziehen*

Riese's explanation of *temporibus* as *suo tempore* seems inadmissible. The sense of the pentameter is suggested by 214. 7 on the same subject: 'muneraque eximius tanti dat liminis auctor / unica continuae praenoscens praemia famae'. In one year the king created a noble structure as a gift for ages to come. *populis,* which may have been taken from 213. 2 'hic pia rex populis Thrasamundus vota dicavit', may have replaced *multis* (cf. Dracont. *Laud. Dei* 3. 704 'post ossa senectae / mortua temporibus multis olimve sepulta') or *longis* (cf. Cic. *Rep.* 2. 59 'non longis temporibus ante'). The former would be the more apt to disappear before *munera*.

212 (Felix)

Aliter

9   maxima sed quisquis patitur fastidia *solis*
          aut gravibus madido corpore torpet aquis,
       hic Thrasamundiacis properet se tinguere thermis:
          protinus effugiet tristis uterque labor.

9 proxima . . . fastigia *L. Mueller*

Disgust with sunshine is a rare disease. Read *molis*. These waters were sovereign for obesity (cf. Cels. 1. 3. 66 'extenuat corpus aqua calida, si quis in eam descendit, magisque si salsa est') and for dropsy. For *moles* = 'corpulence' cf. Nemes. *Cyn.* 161 'ne gravis articulos depravet pondere moles'. In Claud. *Eutr.* 2. 444 a fat man sinks in the mud: 'et pingui suspirat corpore moles / more suis'. Line 11 seems to echo Virg. *Georg.* 2. 481 'quid tantum Oceano properent se tinguere soles / hiberni'.

217 (Felix?)
Epistula. Amans amanti

7   *argento stat* facta manus digitisque tenellis
       serica fila trahens pretioso in stamine ludis.

> 7 facta *ex* firma *A corr.*

A hand made of silver seems a strange item in a catalogue of feminine charms. Read 'argutae stant facta manus'; cf. Ov. *Her.* 10. 60 'facta boum' = ἔργα βοῶν.

23   sed tua labra meo saevum de corde dolorem
       depellant morbumque animae medicaminis huius
       cura fuget, ne tanta putres violentia nervos
       dissecet atque *tuae* moriar pro crimine *causae.*

> 26 causae] curae *Baehrens*

Perhaps *tua . . . causa. pro crimine* seems to mean 'as a reproach (to you)'.

223 (Coronatus)
Locus Virgilianus: 'vivo equidem vitamque extrema per omnia duco'

17   atque domus mihi pontus erat Phrygiique penates
       et quasi iam pirata fui, lacrimisque profusis
       inter aquas † siccabat homo *nostrasque* profecto
       fluctibus *addebant*; fluctus crescebat in astra,
       et mihi naufragium nostri fecere liquores.

> 19 stagnabat humus *Oudendorp*   nostrasque *Oudendorp*: nostroque *A*
> 20 addebat *Oudendorp*   astra *Oudendorp*: astris *A*

Read: 'inter aquas siccabat homo nostrosque profecto / fluctibus addebam'. 'Amidst the waters (i.e. the sea, not *meas lacrimas,* as Riese) a man (myself) was dry (i.e. had no more tears to shed), and I was adding waves of my own to the waves.' For intransitive *sicco,* becoming increasingly frequent from Tertullian on, see L. Feltenius, *Intransitivizations in Latin* (Uppsala, 1977) 124 f.

226 (Coronatus)
Aliter unde supra (i.e. de esiciata)

Mortua fit praedo; pullorum turgida membris
ex aliis crescit nec sese repperit in se.

Punctuate 'mortua fit praedo pullorum; turgida' *sqq.* When dead, the hen takes to preying on chickens, i.e. gets stuffed with them. 'nec sese' = 'et corpora aliena'.

228 (Coronatus)
Unde supra (i.e. de ovata)

Medeam fertur natos Prognenque necasse:
haec natis *atavisque simul vel caede* sororum
crescit; plus moriens sumpsit de *prole* tumorem.

2 haec *Riese*: en *A*: ex *Meyer*   atabisq; *A*   uel *A, sed* ue *in ras.*   sororum
L. Mueller: sorum *A*   3 prole *A*: caede *sched. Divion.*

The subject, a hen stuffed with eggs, is more perspicuously treated in the parallel piece 227 by a different author:

Ovorum copiosa phalanx in ventre tumentis
conditur et membris crescit gallina repletis.
mortua concepit quantum nec viva creavit.

Line 2 presents more problems than one. -*que . . . vel* is suspicious, *atavis* impossible. How could the bird's remote ancestors be involved? And how can she be said to have slaughtered her sister hens? The point must be sought in the comparison with Medea and Procne. They killed only their own children, whereas this hen has consumed not only her own eggs but her sisters' as well: 'haec natis propriisque suis et prole sororum / crescit; plus moriens sumpsit de caede tumorem.'

234 (Pentadius)
De fortuna

17   hostia †*saepe* fuit diri Busiridis hospes,
        Busirisque aris hostia *saepe* fuit.

saepe *(bis) ABV*: saeva *L. Mueller*: et ipse *Heinsius*: lege *Schenkl*: sacra *Baehrens*

Read *caesa.* For the gender agreeing with the predicate cf. Cic. *Man.* 11 'Corinthum patres vestri, totius Graeciae lumen, exstinctum esse voluerunt' (K.–S. I. 42 f.).

23   sola relicta toris flevisti <in> litore, Gnosis;
        laetatur caelo sola relicta toris.

23 flevisti in *vulg.*: fleuisti *ABV*: flevit in *Petschenig*   24 laetaris *nescioquis*

Read *laetata es.*

240
Cupido amans

4   \<*satis*> an \<*mea*> spicula fusa per orbem
vexavere polum laesusque in tempore mundus
invenit poenam?

4 satis et mea add. Wakker

I would prefer *nimis.*

8   licet orbe superno,
Iuppiter, *exultes*; undis, Neptune, tegaris;
abdita poenarum te cingant Tartara, Pluton:
inpositum rumpemus onus!

9 exultes Riese: ex altis A: et salsis Wakker

exultes deserves no comment, and *altis* with *tegaris* is too appropriate to
discard. Perhaps *atque altis.* 'inpositum rumpemus onus' refers only to
Pluto.

15   poenam mundus amet, stupeat, *vincatur,* anhelet!

vincatur Riese: uix (uis sched. Divion.) maior A   anhelet Riese: anhelat A

vincatur is intolerably tame and a transitive verb is required. The only
one I can suggest is *vescatur*; cf. Cic. *Fin.* 5. 57 'paratissimis vesci
voluptatibus'. Both *vesci* and *anhelare* ('pant for') can govern accusatives.

242

9   Aeneidemque suam fac maior †Mincius ornet:
plus fatis possunt Caesaris ora dei.

9 mincius A: mitius V: nuncius codd. recc.

On Augustus' preservation of the Aeneid.

Riese's obelus presumably means that he had something against
Mincius. Baehrens thought that *maior* might be an import from line 7, and
proposed *Aeneidesque (Aeneamque* edd. vett.) *suos* and *vetitis* for *fatis.*
None of this seems at all called for. 'Let Mincius, grown greater, honour his
Aeneid' in peace (cf. Burman: 'Mincius hic ponitur pro ipsa Mantua').

243
De equis aeneis

3   *spirant* aërias *involvere* cursibus auras,
arte citi sed mole graves, properante metallo.

4 sed] nec Baehrens, fort. recte

What is to be made of *spirant involvere*? Perhaps 'sperant . . .
praevertere'; cf. Virg. *Aen.* 12. 345 'equo praevertere ventos' *et sim.*

244
(Thema: Turne, in te suprema salus)

7   nam bella *minatus*
   nunc gerit Aeneas.

7 minatus *Burman*: mutatus *A*

mutatus makes much better sense in the context than *minatus*, which makes little enough. Aeneas was 'transformed' – much more formidable than before. What follows down to line 20 'iam faces, non tela iacit' bears this out. *mŭtatus* keeps company with *tīmendo, ariēte, fāces, fāce.*

253 (Reposianus)
De concubitu Martis et Veneris

The date of this poem is uncertain. Its latest editor, U. Zuccarelli (1972), puts it as early as the end of the second century A.D. I cite from his text.

42   hic rosa cum violis, hic omnis gratia florum,
   hic inter *violas* coma mollis laeta hyacinthi.

43 casias *coni. Baehrens*

As Baehrens noticed, *violas* has been repeated from the previous line. *calthas* is a likely replacement; cf. Virg. *Ecl.* 2. 50 'mollia luteola pingit vaccinia caltha', Ov. *Fast.* 4. 437 'illa legit calthas, huic sunt violaria curae' *et sim.*

55   haec modo purpureum decerpens pollice florem,
   cum delibat eum, suspiria ducat odore;
   ast tibi blanda manus <*florem*> sub pectore condat.

56 delibat eum *Baehrens*: diligatum *codd.*: delibato *Klapp: alii alia*   odore *coni.*
Wernsdorf: odorem *vel sim. codd.*   57 florem *add. Zuccarelli*: flores *Riese*: tenero
Wernsdorf: alii alia

Translators notwithstanding, *haec* and *tibi* (and *tu* in the next line) refer to different attendants of Venus. The missing word in 57 is probably the name of a particular flower, corresponding to *purpureum florem* (i.e. *hyacinthum*) in the previous line and the roses and lilies preceding. *violas* is the most obvious.

64   his igitur lucis Paphie, dum proelia Mavors
   horrida, dum populos diro terrore fatigat,
   ludebat.

65 horrida *cum obelo Riese,* vorsat *coniciens*

According to Zuccarelli, *fatigat* 'congiunto con "proelia" appare un accoppiamento ardito'. But cf. Sil. 7. 492 'hic dabit ex sese qui tertia bella fatiget'. For the Virgilian cliché 'horrida proelia' see *Thes.* VI. 2994. 50 (*sim. horrida bella. arma*).

109   stringebat *Paphiae Mavors tunc pectore dextram*
et collo innexam ne laedant pondera laevam,
lilia cum roseis supponit candida sertis.

109 pectora dextra Oudendorp

This text has stimulated translators to some remarkable acrobatics.
J.W. and A.M. Duff (Loeb, *Minor Latin Poets*) make Mars draw his right
hand from the Paphian's breast and then take precautions 'lest his weight
should hurt the left arm twined around her neck'. For Zuccarelli Mars
executes a different manoeuvre: 'Premeva Marte in quegli istanti la sua
destra sul seno di Pafie e, perchè il peso dei due corpi non facesse male al
suo braccio sinistro' etc. Oudendorp's conjecture, adopted by Riese, is
right as far as it goes; but Mars afraid that Venus' weight might be too
much for his left is a figure of comedy, which this author did not intend.
Read: 'stringebat Paphie Mavortis pectora dextra'. The whole action is
appropriate to Venus (with recollections of Lucretius), and she is the
subject of the following lines, 112 f. In 113 ff. it is Mars who falls asleep,
with Venus' arms supporting him (121).

123   non omnis resupina iacet, sed corpore flexo
molliter et laterum qua se confinia *iungant.*

125   Martem respiciens, deponit lumina somno,
sed gratiosa, decens . . . pro lucis forte Cupido
Martis tela *regens*

124 iungant *Maehly*: iungunt *codd.*   126 *post* decens *lac. stat.*
Baehrens   pro lucis] proludit *vel* praeludit *Oudendorp*: proludens *vel* pro ludis
Burman   127 regit *Roncoroni*: gerit *Riese*

However 123 f. is interpreted, the manuscript reading seems preferable
('but with a gentle bend of her body where side meets side' the Duffs). The
sentence might well end with 125. What follows is doubtless much
corrupted. It may have run: 'somnia grata decent. prope ludit forte Cupido
/ Martis tela gerens'.

159   haeserat Ignipotens, stupefactus crimine tanto;
iam quasi *torpescens* – vix sufficit ira dolori –
ore fremit *maestoque modo gemit* ultima pulsans
ilia et indignans suspiria pressa fatigat.

160 turpescens codd.   162 maestoque Burman: maestus codd.

Read: 'fervescens . . . ore fremit, maestus modo congemit'. For 'modo' =
'postmodo' see Housman on Manil. 1. 871.

254 (Felix)
Postulatio honoris aput Victorianum virum inlustrem et primiscriniarium

29   sit mihi fas audire sacros et cernere cultus,
      ecclesiae spectans dona venire mea.

30 exspectans Burman: 'corruptus; num ecclesia spero?' Baehrens

The writer begs to be made a priest. Line 30 means 'beholding gifts come to the church as mine', i.e. sharing in them. Cf. Eugen. Tolet. *Satisfactio* 23 (Vollmer, p. 115) 'unde mihi possent dona venire simul'.

255
Thema Vergilianum: 'Nec tibi diva parens'

Dedecus o iuvenem turpisque infamia Teucrum,
qui segnis per bella *lates,* †*gens* perfida *et amens*
non virtute potens, *non belli* maximus auctor,
ignavus tu semper eris semperque fuisti.

2 lates Riese: fores A: iaces Baehrens   gens] mens Oudendorp

Line 2 is evidently much corrupted. Timpanaro (*SIFC* 25 (1951) 40) defends *gens* as alluding to Laomedon, comparing *Aen.* 10. 228 'deum gens, / Aenea'). But that allusion is brought in later on as though for the first time; see below. *fores* is admittedly senseless, and neither *amens* nor *non belli maximus auctor* bears a moment's scrutiny. This a case of nothing venture, nothing have. The following reconstruction is less arbitrary than it may at first sight appear: 'cui segnis per bella manus, mens perfida; fraude, / non virtute potens, metuendi maximus auctor'. For the last phrase cf. Tac. *Ann.* 2. 33. 6 'nec . . . defuturum corrigendi auctorem' *et sim.*

6   nec *non* est aliud, quod maius crimen obibis.
      iamque tuo generi quia semper *perfidus* extas,
      non equidem miror. non est ex tempore natum;
      antiquos imitaris avos, periuria patrum.

In line 6 read *nunc* for *non.* Aeneas can do nothing now worse than what he has done already. In line 7 the description 'treacherous to your own race' is inapplicable. For *perfidus* perhaps read *proximus,* i.e. *simillimus*; cf. Ov. *Met.* 12. 397 'cervix umerique manusque / pectoraque artificum laudatis proxima signis', 14.509 'ut non cycnorum, sic albis proxima cycnis'.

271 (Regianus)

Ante bonam Venerem gelidae *per* litora Baiae.
illa natare lacus cum lampade iussit Amorem.
dum natat, algentes cecidit scintilla per undas;
hinc vapor ussit aquas: quicumque natavit, amavit.

The full stop after line 1 is missing in Riese. In the same line 'gelidae per litora Baiae' is poor stuff, unworthy of this graceful little composition. I suspect that it originally ran: 'ante bonam Venerem gelidae, mala litora, Baiae'.

279 (Vincentius)
Phaedra

10   ne metuas facinus! 'non vult hoc scire Cupido'.

The quotation marks, whatever their purpose, should disappear. Phaedra tells Hippolytus not to be afraid of committing a crime by acceding to her plea. The love-god does not want to know anything about that, i.e. he does not care.

286 (Symphosius)
Aenigmata

The Riddles of Symphosius, each consisting of three hexameters, are generally assigned to the late fourth or early fifth century. They were last edited in a doctoral thesis by R.T. Ohl (Philadelphia, 1928). The collection survives complete in sixteen MSS (and partially in four others), of which the Salmasianus (A) is the most important. The others are divided into two families, B and D, representing separate recensions. β and w are the most important in the first, d, a, and h in the second.

Riese's text is influenced by an unfounded theory of the transmission. I cite from Ohl's.

III   Anulus cum gemma

Corporis extremi non *magnum* pondus adhaesi.
ingenitum dicas, ita pondere nemo gravatur;
una tamen facies plures habitura figuras.

3 habet ore *Riese*

If the weight was small, why *should* anyone find it oppressive? Read *non parvum*. 'Thus does an author suffer when a stupid scribe thinks himself clever' (see Housman, *Classical papers* 594 and cf. his note on Juv. 10. 351; also, on 'polar' errors, C. Kopff, *AJP* 96 (1975) 117 ff.). For a heavy ring cf. Mart. 11. 37.

It is not enough to defend *habitura,* as Ohl does, with a reference to *Aenigm.* V. 1 'nexa ligor ferro, multos habitura ligatos'. *adhaesi* has to be the main verb to which *habitura* is subordinate. Thus:

Corporis extremi non parvum pondus adhaesi
(ingenitum dicas, ita pondere nemo gravatur),
una tamen facies plures habitura figuras.

I.e. 'una facies, plures tamen h. f.'

VIII   Nebula

> Nox ego sum facie, sed non sum nigra colore,
> inque die media tenebras tamen affero mecum;
> nec mihi dant stellae *lucem* nec Cynthia *lumen.*

3 lucem . . . lumen *D*: lumen . . . lucem *AB*

Ohl's notion that '*lux* seems to have been applied oftener to the light of the sun and stars and *lumen* to that of the moon' belongs to the latter sort of illumination. His citations are easily capped by others making the opposite way. Read: 'nec mihi dant stellae lumen nec Cynthia nocte'.

IX   Pluvia

> Ex alto venio longa delapsa ruina;
> de caelo cecidi medias *transmissa* per auras;
> sed sinus excepit, qui *me* simul ipse recepit.

2 transmissa *D*: dimissas *A*: dimissa *B*: demissa *s*: si missa *Baehrens*   3 simul] prius *Heinsius*

demissa should be read in line 2; cf. Lucr. 6. 496 'in terras demissus ut imber / decidat'. Ohl's translation of line 3, 'but earth's bosom has taken me in, as soon as it has retaken me', is no more helpful than his comment, 'Symphosius is especially fond of such word-play in the third line'. Read *se* for *me*. Rain-water comes, at least in part, originally from the sea (and rivers; cf. Lucr. 6. 503 ff., Manil. 2. 75). Some of it falls back into the water, which in receiving the rain has at the same time recovered its substance.

XVIII   Coclea

> Porto domum mecum, semper migrare parata,
> mutatoque solo non sum miserabilis exul,
> sed *mihi concilium* de caelo nascitur ipso.

3 consilium *s*: conchilium *cod. Parisinus 8088*: conchylium *Castalio*

No more words need be wasted on a meaningless text or a conjecture which violates metre without restoring sense. I suspect that line 3 began originally 'sed genitale solum'. The snail is on his native (i.e. home) ground wherever he wanders, for his shell, the 'sky' that covers him, makes any ground his *patria.*

XIX   Rana

> Raucisonans ego sum media vocalis in unda,
> sed vox laude *sonat, quasi* se quoque laudet et ipsa;
> cumque canam semper, nullus mea carmina laudat.

2 sed non 1. s. vox, quae se *Schenkl*   caret, quae se laudaverit *Heumann*   vox rauca sonat, quasi se conlaudet *coni. Riese*   sonat] vacat *Heinsius*

Following the pointer in line 3 read: 'sed vox laude vacat, nisi se' *sqq.*

XXIV   Curculio

> Non bonus agricolis, non frugibus utilis hospes,
> non magnus forma, non *recto* nomine dictus,
> non gratus Cereri non parvam sumo saginam.

'Non recto nomine dictus': why? The explanations of early editors are all either far-fetched or pointless . . . . Possibly the point lies in the variant spelling, *c* versus *g*' (i.e. *curculio* / *gurgulio*). So Ohl, who, like Gesner before him, found the right track but failed to pursue it. For *recto* read *certo*, which is cited by Wernsdorf from Besuelus' edition of 1563.

XXVI   Grus

> Littera sum caeli penna perscripta volanti,
> bella cruenta gerens volucri discrimine Martis;
> non vereor pugnas, dum non sit *longior* hostis.

            3 longius *A*

longulus? See above on 199. 88.

XLII   Beta

> Tota vocor Graece, *sed* non sum tota Latine.

        tota *D*: beta *AB*   sum tota *D*: sum tobeta *A*: sum beta *B*

The word *beta*, meaning 'beet', *does* exist in Latin. But as the name of the second letter of the alphabet *beta* (Greek) is curtailed to *be*. This could be expressed by substituting *quod* for *sed*: 'What I am in Latin when incomplete (*non tota*), I am called in Greek complete'.

LXXVIII   Scalae

> Nos sumus, ad caelum quae scandimus, alta petentes,
> concordi fabrica quas unus continet ordo,
> ut simul haerentes *per nos comitentur* ad auras.

         3 per nos nitantur *Buenemann*: nos connitamur *Schenkl*

Buenemann's conjecture was accepted by Baehrens and Riese. Symphosius wrote *pronos comitemur*. The rungs of the ladder (rather than steps of the flight of stairs) collectively (cf. *scandimus*) accompany the climbers, who cling to them bending forward.

LXXX   Tintinnabulum

> 3   non resono positus, *motus quoque* saepe resulto.

      motus quoque saepe β: motus quoque longe *A*: motus longeque *Castalio (Baehrens)*: sed motus saepe *Schenkl (Riese)*

Perhaps *commotus saepe. quoque*, which Ohl explains as 'simply used rather loosely with conjunctive force' and translates 'however', appears to be an interpolation in replacement of a lost half-foot. *saepe* refers to the repeated strokes of the clapper; not 'I often ring out'.

LXXXI   Lagena

> Mater erat Tellus, genitor est ipse Prometheus;
> auriculaeque *regunt redimitam* ventre cavato.
> dum *misere cecidi* mater mea me laniavit.

2 que *non habent* *Aβ*   rigent *Froehner*   redimitam *Pithoeus*: -to *codd. plerique*
(Riese): -ta β: -tae *Perionius*: geminatae *Baehrens*   3 misere (-ra *Aβwh*) cecidi (-dit
A) *AB*: cecidi subito *D (Riese)*   mea mater β   laniavit] diuisit *Aβ*   divisit
me mea mater *Baehrens*

In line 2 I suggest 'auriculae surgunt redimitae'; in 3 'dum cecidi, miseram'. The piece offers a lagoena with two handles. Usually they seem to have had one (cf. Marquardt, *Röm. Privatleben* 649).

LXXXVIII   Strigilis aenea

> †Rubida† *curva capax,* alienis humida guttis,
> luminibus falsis auri mentita colorem,
> dedita sudori, modico subcumbo labori.

1 rubida *D*: rubea *AB*: roscida *Castalio*: uvida *vel* rufeo *Wernsdorf*: Cuprea *Baehrens*:
aerea *coni. Riese*   2 mentita colorem *D*: simulata metallo *B*: simulata metallo
mentita colorem *A*

' "rubida" is a comparatively rare word, yet Symphosius is so uniformly careful of his language and meter that it is hard to conceive of his not knowing the quantity of the first syllable.' So Ohl, who remarks that 'the many emendations proposed, with the possible exception of Wernsdorf's "uvida", have little *raison d'être* other than the caprice of their authors'. The solution is *rubra, recurva.* But the next epithet, *capax,* could hardly be more incongruous: *rapax* fits (I would read *rapaces* with Barth in Luc. I. 461). In line 3 Ohl explains that the phrase 'modico subcumbo labori', 'which might more properly be said of the person who has exercised to the point of perspiration, is here applied to the strigil itself', adding that 'too vigorous a use of the scraper might work harm'. This is confused but right in part. The strigil 'succumbs to little toil' because the person using it must not work it too hard. But the point is in the contrast with 'dedita sudori', which would normally mean 'devoted to labour'. Although 'dedicated to sweat' (i.e. to removing sweat from the body), the strigil none the less is soon exhausted.

XCI   Pecunia

> Terra fui primo, latebris abscondita terrae;
> nunc aliud pretium flammae nomenque dederunt,
> nec iam terra vocor, licet ex me terra paretur.

1 terrae *D*: diris *AB*: duris *cod. Parisinus 8319 (Baehrens)*

Line 3 is correctly explained by Ohl (after Heumann): the coin is no longer called earth (as when it was ore), though it is used to buy earth (land). The first two lines should be repunctuated: 'Terra fui primo latebris abscondita terrae, / nunc aliud (*sc.* 'sum'). pretium' *sqq.* Fire, i.e. the smelting and minting process, gave the ore value and a name of its own ('denarius' *vel sim.*).

XCII   Mulier quae geminos pariebat

Plus ego sustinui quam corpus debuit unum.
tres animas habui, quas omnes intus *habebam*:
discessere duae, sed tertia paene peregit.

2 alebam *Baehrens*   3 abscessere *Baehrens*   poene *cod. Sangallensis 273*:
poena β: pena *A*   peregit *AB*: secuta est *D* (*Riese*)

alebam, to which Ohl for some reason adds a pejorative exclamation mark, is to be accepted; cf. 190. 7 above. In line 3 *secuta est* is clearly a substitute for the difficult *peregit,* which Ohl interprets in the unparalleled sense 'died'. *fata peregit* would be easy, but the woman's death is not mentioned in the title. If *peregit* is sound, *me* has to be understood and the point lies in a paradox: the third life (her own) was nearly the death of her. But *perivit,* suggested to me by Professor C.P. Jones, may very well be right (cf. Neue-Wagener. *Formenlehre*[3] III. 440).

XCIII   Miles podagricus

Bellipotens olim, saevis metuendus in armis,
quinque pedes habui, *quod* numquam nemo negavit.
nunc mihi vix duo sunt; inopem me copia fecit.

1 saeuis *BD*: semper *A*   2 quinque] sex *Aβwh*   quos *B*   3 fecit *D*:
reddit *AB*

Both of the interpretations discussed in Ohl's note are patently wrong, though Castalio rightly perceived that there is a play on two meanings of *pes.* The gouty old soldier will have been a centurion, *castrorum metator* like Decidius Saxa, i.e. *decempedator*; cf. Veget. *Mil.* 3. 8 'opus vero centuriones decempedis metiuntur'. In those days he had ten feet, i.e. a ten-foot rod (the two he walked on are ignored). Now he has barely two, a fact which he blames upon his service (commentators point out that 'inopem me copia fecit' comes from Ov. *Met.* 3. 466). Line 2 should therefore read: 'quinque pedes habui bis, numquam nemo negavit'. *bis* would easily drop out after *-bui.* For its position cf. Manil. 3. 597 'imaque tricenos bis fundamenta per annos'.

XCIV   Luscus alium vendens

Cernere iam fas est quod vix tibi credere fas est:
unus inest oculus, capitum sed milia *multa.*

qui quod habet vendit, quod non habet unde parabit?

tit. alium vendens *Pithoeus*: alios uendens (uind- *A*) *codd. paene omnes* (*Baehrens*): alium tenens *sched. Divion.* (*Riese*)

Line 2 is unintelligible. The heads of the garlic cannot 'be in' the one-eyed man; he is selling them, and this needs stating so as to prepare for the question in line 3. *multa* must be replaced by *vendit*. The man sells thousands of heads (of garlic). If he sells the heads he has, where will he find the head he needs, i.e. one with two eyes?

291 (Luxorius)
Trochaicum de piscibus, qui ab hominibus cibos capiebant

5   odit ardui procellas et dolosi gurgitis,
       ac suum, *quo libet* esse, transnatans *colit* mare.
       sic famem gestu loquaci *et* mitiori †vertice
       discit ille quam sit aptum ventris arte vincere.

6 libet *Maehly*: liber *A*   colit *Duebner*: solet *A*   8 aptus *Meyer*

An elaborate edition of the early sixth-century African epigrammatist Luxorius by M. Rosenblum appeared in 1961 (*Luxorius, a Latin poet among the Vandals*). In 1963 F. Kurucz and I.K. Horvàth published a text and Hungarian translation in *Act. ant. et arch.* (VI) of the University Attila József. The text is based on Baehrens (!), but some account is taken of an unpublished edition by H. Happ (Diss. Tübingen, 1958). A number of passages are treated in an article by V. Tandoi (*RFIC* 98 (1970) 37-63). Luxorius' text and interpretation cannot be said to have profited significantly from these activities.

For previous attempts to deal with line 6 of this epigram it is enough to refer to Tandoi's discussion (l.c. 40 f.). All that is required is to remove *quo* and write *libenter* for *liber*: 'ac suum libenter esse transnatans solet mare'. For *libenter esse* see Nägelsbach-Müller, *Lat. Stilistik*[9] 618. The fish is happy swimming across his private sea, i.e. his pool.

Baehrens and Riese regard 7-8 as unintelligible, as indeed they are; but the only change necessary is from *et* to *in*: 'sic ille in mitiori vertice gestu loquaci discit quam sit aptum ventris famem arte vincere.' For *mitiori,* which may refer to the absence of salt as well as of turbulence, cf. Sen. *N. Q.* 3. 14. 3 'quomodo maris sic et huius aquae mitioris.'

297 (Luxorius)
Phalaecium in moechum, quod debriatus plorabat, cum coitum inplere
non posset

3   effundis lacrimas, quod esse moechus
       multo non valeas mero subactus.

5   *plura* ne futuas, peto, Lucine,
        aut semper bibe taediumque plange,
        aut, numquam ut futuas, venena sume.

5 plura *Riese*: plora *A*   6 aut *Meyer*: et *A*   bibe taediumque plange *Meyer*:
uiuit odiumq; plangit *A*

Taking *ne futuas* as a command, I would read: 'plora, ne futuas, peto,
Lucine, / et semper bibe taediumque plange; / aut' *sqq.*

298 (Luxorius)
In spadonem regium, qui mitellam sumebat

5   proprii memor pudoris,
        bene conscius quid esset,
        posuit cogente nullo,
        fuerat minus quod illi.

The *mitella* will have been in the shape of a phallus.

299 (Luxorius)
Anapaesticum in magum mendicum

9   *qui puto quod* peius
        egeas totum semper in *orbem,*
        mage, si *posces* membra perempta.

9 qui *Baehrens*: q; *A*   peius *Baehrens*: petus *A*: petas *sched. Divion.*: penus
Petschenig   10 in aevum *Baehrens*   11 posces *Riese*: poscis *A*

This magician haunts graveyards (3 'ire per umbras atque sepulcra /
pectore egeno titubans gestis'). Why does he not feed (lit. 'graze') on
corpses through all eternity? 'quid, peto, quo peius / egeas, totum semper
in aevum, / mage, si pascis membra perempta?' (alternatively 'quin . . .
depascis').

302 (Luxorius)
In medicolenonem

7   at tu fornice turpius vacabas,
        exercens aliis, quod ipse possis
        lenatis melius tibi puellis
10   scortandi solito labore ferre.
        novi, quid libeat tuum, chirurge,
        conspectos animum videre cunnos:
        vis ostendere te minus virum esse,
        arrectos satis est mares videre.

11 novi *vulg.*: nobi *A*   libeat *Burman*: liberat *A*: iubeat *Baehrens*   12
conspectos] conlectos *Maehly*

Lines 7-10 mean that the doctor supplied other men with the girls he procured, whereas he might, as a practised *cinaedus,* have met their needs himself better than the girls could do. *quod* (= *mentulam*) is object of *exercens* (so no comma), and *puellis* is abl. of comparison: 'facis ut alii exerceant id quod ipse melius ferre possis quam puellae quas lenavisti.' Line 13 should end with a full stop: 'novi quid (= cur) tuum animum libeat (for the accusative see *Thes.* VII. 2. 1326. 12) videre cunnos quos (eodem tempore) conspiciunt alii viri.' He does it to show that he is a *cinaedus.* The women are in full view, but he contents himself with watching the excited males.

304 (Luxorius)
De turre in viridario posita, ubi se Fridamal aprum pinxit occidere

17   hic spumantis apri iaculo post terga retorto
       frontem et cum geminis naribus ora feris.
       ante ictum subita prostrata est belua morte,
20   cui prius extingui quam cecidisse fuit.
       iussit fata manus telo, nec vulnera sensit
       exerrans anima iam pereunte cruor.

19 actutum *Petschenig*: adque ictum *Baehrens*   21 misit *Petschenig*

The background is not altogether clear. The boar in the picture is dying from a spear-stroke, but the spear is invisible. Apparently Fridamal has recovered it and is holding it behind his back (17). At any rate the poet allows himself the puerile conceit that the boar died *before* he was hit – the death is in the picture, but no stroke. Line 21 should be repunctuated: 'iussit fata manus, telo nec vulnera sensit'. A hand (the painter's) ordained the death, but the bleeding animal (*cruor*) felt no wound.

306 (Luxorius)
In aurigam senem victum crimina in populos iactantem

Te quotiens victum circus, Cyriace, resultat
   crimine victores polluis et populos.
non visum quereris senio languente perisse
   castigasque tuae tarda flagella manus.

3 non *Riese*: tunc *A*: quin *Baehrens*

tunc is more likely to have arisen from *nec,* or perhaps from *tu nec,* after *tu* had crept in from *te* in line 1.

307 (Luxorius)
In podagrum venationi studentem

4   esse inter iuvenes cupit, vocari
           baudus, dum misero gemat dolore
           et nil *praevaleat.*

                   6 praevaleat *Burman*: proualeat *A*

Read *par valeat* (sc. *iuvenibus*).

308 (Luxorius)

In supra scriptum, quod multa scorta habuit et eas custodiebat

           Zelo <agitas> plures, *Incurvus, clune* puellas,
               sed nulla est, quae te sentiat esse virum.
           custodis clausas, tamquam sis omnibus aptus;
               est tamen internus Iuppiter ex famulis.
5   si nihil ergo vales, †*vacuo* cur arrigis †*oge*
           et facis ignavus mentis adulterium?

1 zelo agitas *Riese*: zelo *A*: zelotypus *Salmasius*: zelaris *Baehrens*   Incurvus *Riese ex*
307. 2: incurbas *A*: incurva *Baehrens*   clune *vulg.*: plune *A*   5 uacuo *A*:
vacua *vulg.*: vanum *Baehrens*: vana *L. Mueller*   oge *A*: orge *Heinsius*: arte *Burman*:
inguen *Baehrens*: orche *coni. Riese*   6 ignavus *L. Mueller*: ignarus *A*

Apart from Riese's conjecture nothing but the title connects this poem
with the preceding, and these titles are not to be trusted; cf. on 312 and 365.
The author of this one was evidently misled by *incurbas* (did he too read
Incurvus?).

In the first line try: 'zelo <typo> plures incursas pene puellas'. *plune* in A
is explained by *plures*. In line 5 read: 'vacuum . . . inguen'. *vacuum* amounts
to *vanum*; see my defence of Coripp. *Ioh.* 5. 13 'congressus vacuis ductor
fortissimus armis' in *Gnomon* 43 (1971) 519, later reinforced by Ps.-Quint.
Decl. Mai. (Lehnert) 71. 19 'vacua circa me tela ceciderunt' (*HSPh* 80
(1976) 193).

I take occasion to point out another correlation: *Anth. Lat.* 286. XI
(Symphosius) 'pulvis aquae tenuis modico cum pondere lapsus' with my
conjecture in Paulin. Nol. *Carm.* 18. 18 'cinerosis nubibus' (*AJPh* 97 (1976)
9).

309 (Luxorius)

Anacreontium in medicum inpotentem, qui ter viduam duxit uxorem

11   iam *nosco,* cui videtur
           nupsisse Paula rursus.
           nulli! quid ergo fecit?
           mutare mox lugubrem
15   quam sumpserat cupivit
           uxor nefanda vestem,

ut quartus atque – quintus
possit venire coniunx!

11 nosco] agnosco *Baehrens*

Read: 'iam posco: cui videtur / nupsisse Paula rursus? / nulli' (*sc.*
videtur). Or *posco* may be parenthetic; cf. Eugen. Tolet. *Carm.* 35. 5 'da
guttas oculis, posco, da verba querellis'. I do not know what the dash in
line 17 was supposed to convey. The meaning is: 'Paula has not married a
fourth time; *this* husband does not count. She merely wanted to get out of
mourning so as to attract a fourth (real) husband and, in due course, a
fifth.'

312 (Luxorius)
De Fama picta in stabulo circi

Qualem te pictor stabulis formavit equorum,
    talem te nostris blanda referto iugis.
semper et adsiduo vincendi munera porta
    his quorum limen fortis amica sedes.

4 sedes *vulg.*: sedis *A*: tenes *Meyer*

This piece is conclusive proof, even if there were no other, that the titles
do not go back to Luxorius, at any rate not all of them; see Rosenblum, pp.
65 ff. *Fama* in this one is an error deriving from the following epigram. The
subject of the painting here was Victoria.

313 (Luxorius)
Aliter

Verum, Fama, tibi vultum pictura notavit,
    dum vivos oculos iuncea forma gerit.
tu quamvis totum velox rapiaris in orbem,
    pulcrior hoc uno limine clausa sedes.

2 vivos] vigiles *Baehrens*

The first couplet is a question. The poet would hardly state on his own
authority that the picture of Fame was a true likeness.

314 (Luxorius)
In vicinum invidum

Zeleris nimium cur mea, Marcie,
tamquam si pereas, limina, nescio,
cum *sis* proximior, una velut domus,
et *nostros* paries dimidiet lares.

3 sis *vulg.*: sit *A*   une *L. Mueller*   domus *Meyer*: domu *A*

Lines 3 f. are problematic. Reading *sis* (or *sim*?) for *sit* we are to suppose that Marcius (on the vocative *Marcie,* repeated in line 8, see Neue-Wagener, *Formenlehre*[3] I. 127) and the poet lived in adjoining semidetached houses. That is presented as a reason why Marcius ought not to be jealous – it makes no difference whether *cum* is causal, expressing the poet's perplexity, or concessive. Now surely a man is *more* likely to be jealous of an immediate neighbour than of someone further away. Perhaps *sit* is to be retained and *vestros* read for *nostros* in line 4: 'cum' ('although') 'sit proximior, una velut, domus / et vestros' *sqq.* This also removes the awkwardness of *una domus* in apposition to *proximior* (masc.).

316 (Luxorius)
De eo qui se poetam dicebat quod in triviis cantaret et a pueris laudaretur

6   hoc *nostrae* faciunt semper et alites:
        ni rite *instituistes, sibila tum* canunt.

6 hoc *vulg.*: huc *A*   nostrae] rostro *Burman*: notae *Baehrens*   alites *vulg.*: aliter *A*   7 nil *vulg.*: nih *A*   instituies *Riese ('i.e. eas docebis'!)*: incapies *A*   nil recti in capite est, s. t. c. *Petschenig*

This poetaster is described in the preceding lines as noisily reciting his uncouth and malicious compositions at street corners (read *iocis* (L. Mueller) for *locis* in line 3). Therein he behaves just like birds of ill omen: 'hoc nigrae faciunt semper et alites: / nil rite incipias sibila cum canunt'. For *nigrae* cf. Ov. *Am.* 3. 12. 1 'quis fuit ille dies, quo tristia semper amanti / omina non albae concinuistis aves?' 'incipias' = 'incipitur' (K.-S. I. 653 f.).

317 (Luxorius)
In puellam hermaphroditam

      Monstrum feminei bimembre sexus,
      quam coacta virum facit libido,
      quin gaudes futui furente cunno?
      cur te decipit inpotens voluptas?
5   non *das* quo pateris facisque, cunnum.
      illam, qua mulier probaris esse,
      partem cum dederis, puella tunc sis.

3 quin *Baehrens*: quae *A*   4 cur *vulg.*: quur *A*: cum *Burman*   4 decipit *Riese*: cępit *A*: cepit ita *Baehrens*   5 das *vulg.*: des *A*   cunnum] damnum *Baehrens*   6 qua *vulg.*: quam *A*   7 tunc sis *Burman*: tunc is *A*: tunc fis *Baehrens*

The unnatural lust of line 2 (cf. Plin. *N. H.* 33. 62 'haec enim inventio eius (sc. *auri*) naturalis est; alia, quam dicemus, coacta') is not the bisexual girl's

but that of the women who make her play a masculine role. Read: 'quae
gaudet futui furente cunno, cur te decipit . . .?' The change of *des* to *das* in
line 5 is a further product of incomprehension. The girl is told that she
should not *dare cunnum* both actively and passively. When 'giving' that
part of herself which proves her to be a woman, let her *be* a woman. Cf.
Mart. 12. 96. 12 'cede sua pueris, utere parte tua'.

318 (Luxorius)
Ad eum qui per diem dormiens noctu vigilabat

Stertis anhelanti fessus quod corde, Lycaon,
  exhorrens lucis munera *parta die.*

2 parta *ABV*: grata *Baehrens*: sparsa *Petschenig*   die *Petschenig*: dei *ABV*: diei
Meyer: piae *Baehrens*

Read 'munera grata dei', taking *lucis* with *dei* as in Tertull. *Adv. Marc.* 2.
29 'alium deum lucis ostendisse debueras, alium vero tenebrarum'.
Luxorius seems to have been at least nominally a Christian (cf. Levy, *RE*
XIII. 2104. 44), though Rosenblum (pp. 45 ff.) considers this unproven.

322 (Luxorius)
De eo qui uxorem suam prostare faciebat pro filiis habendis

Stirpe negata patrium nomen
non pater audis; *carus* adulter
coiugis castae viscera damnas,
pariat spurios ut tibi natos,
5   inscia, quo sint semine creti.
fuerant forsan ista ferenda
foeda, Proconi, vota parumper,
†*scire* vel *ipsa* si tuus umquam
†posset adultus dicere matrem.

2 carus] rarus *Klapp*: pactus *Baehrens*   3 damnas] aravit *Baehrens*   9
si tuus *L. Mueller*: situs (i *supra lin.*) *A*   ipsa . . . matrem] ipsum . . . patrem *Baehrens*

Read *castus* in line 2. This husband is an adulterer because the men who
sleep with his wife do so by his agency; but he is also chaste, because he
does not sleep with her himself. She for her part, though an adulteress in
literal fact, is chaste because her husband, not herself, is really responsible.

In line 9 for *scire vel ipsa* read *ille vel ipsam.* The husband's proceeding
might have been tolerable if a (nominal) son of his when grown up could
refer even to his mother, i.e. if the husband had managed matters so as not
publicly to disgrace his wife. As it was, his 'sons' in later life would not only
be unable to name their (real) fathers; they would have to keep quiet about
their mother (whose name they did know) as well.

323 (Luxorius)
De aleatore in pretio lenocinii ludente

Ludis, nec superas, Ultor, ad aleam,
nec quicquam in tabula das, nisi virginem,
spondens blanditias et coitus simul.
hoc cur das aliis, quod poteras tibi?
5   an *tali melius praemia* grata sunt?
aut prodest vitium tale quod *impetras*?
si vincas, ego te non puto virginem
in luxum cupere, sed mage vendere.

5 an] hau *Baehrens*   tali *L. Mueller*: tabulae *A*: tablae *Schubert*   praemia]
proelia *Schubert*   6 aut] at *Baehrens*   impetras *L. Mueller*: imperas
A2   8 capere *Baehrens, fort. recte*

Line 5 may have run: 'an tantum tabulae proelia grata sunt?', i.e. did Ultor care only for *proelia aleatoria,* not for *proelia amatoria*? *tantum* having fallen out before *tabulae, melius* (for *potius, magis*) might be added to fill the verse. In the next line *imperas* seems to have replaced *impetrat*: 'or perhaps the vice (of gambling), which makes such a demand of you (*quod tale impetrat*), really works to your advantage?' If Ultor had not been obliged to use the girl in this way, he would have sold her – an admission of impotence.

324 (Luxorius)
In nomen Aegyptii, quo equi circi infortunium capiebant

5   tu quoque *confractis defectus* in *aequore* pinnis,
      Icare, Phoebeo victus ab igne cadis.

5 compactis *Klapp*   aequora *Petschenig*

Read: 'confectis deiectus in aequora'. For *confectis pinnis* cf. Suet. *Cal.* 1. 2 'cuius (cordis) ea natura existimatur ut tinctum veneno igne confici nequeat'.

326 (Luxorius)
De eo qui amicos ad prandium clamabat, ut plura exposceret xenia

Gaudeo quod me nimis ac frequenter
ambitu pascis, Blumarit, superbo.
unde sed pascor? mea sunt per omnes
sparsa convivas bona. nec volebam,
5   pasceres quemquam peteresque mecum,
ne tibi quicquam detur, unde pascas.
hoc tamen sed si vitio teneris,
me precor numquam iubeas vocari.

2 *et* 5 poscis *et* posceres *Baehrens*

This is an unusually obscure piece. The poet complains that Blumarit's repeated invitations to dinner mean that he has to give his host expensive presents. It is *his* money which Blumarit uses to feed his guests. Presumably the *xenia* were sold to pay for the meals. But why were the other guests not similarly laid under contribution (note *amicos* in the title)? Lines 4-6 seem to mean: 'I didn't want you to entertain anybody and had rather you had asked me *not* to give you anything for that purpose'. With 'peteresque mecum' (cf. *Thes.* IV. 1371. 73) understand 'sed volebam.'

329 (Luxorius)
In eum qui foedas amabat

Diligit informes et foedas Myrro puellas;
    quas *aliter* pulcro viderit ore, timet.

2 aliter *vulg.*: alitet *A*: suavi et *coni. Riese*   viderit *Salmasius*: vident *A*

Read 'quas medio aut'. *medio* dropping out, *aut* became *alit,* which was expanded to *alit. et.*

336 (Luxorius)
In aurigam effeminatum numquam vincentem

Praecedis, Vico, nec tamen praecedis,
et quam debueras tenere partem,
hac mollis misero teneris usu.
umquam vincere possis ut quadrigis,
5   corruptor tibi sit retro ponendus.

1 precedis (*prius*) *A*: procedis *Meyer*   2 qua d. vigere parte *Maehly*   3
misero *Burman*: misera *A*

Riese's text is faultless, but his comment on the first line, 'ambigue dictum: ire pergis, nec tamen ceteros superas', creates a presumption that he was equally far from understanding the other four.

Praecedis (*sc.* percidenti) nec tamen praecedis (*sc.* in quadrigarum certaminibus). Culo, quem debueras clausum tenere, teneris (i.e. pathicus inservis). Ut aliquando quadrigis vincere possis, corruptor tibi retro sit ponendus (*sc.* qui tibi praecedere (praetervehi) nolit).

338 (Luxorius)
De funere mulieris formosae, quae litigiosa fuit

Gorgoneos vultus habuit Catucia coniunx:
    haec dum pulcra foret, iurgia saepe dabat.
fecerat atque suum semper rixando maritum,
    esset ut *insano* stultius *ore* tacens.

5   et quotiens illam trepido cernebat amore,
           horrebat, tamquam vera Medusa foret.
           defuncta est tandem, haec iurgia ferre per umbras
           cumque ipsa litem reddere *Persephone.*

3 suum *sched. Divion.:* om. *A:* eadem *Baehrens*   5 illam *Burman:* illa
A   amore *'suspectum' iudice Baehrens*   6 horrebat *Maehly:* haerebat
A   8 Persephone *Heinsius:* persenecem *A*

This miserable botch was once a neat epigram, quite up to Martial's
average:

           Gorgoneos vultus habuit Catucia coniunx;
                haec, dum pulcra foret, iurgia saepe dabat,
           fecerat atque suum semper rixando maritum
                esset ut infanti stultius aere tacens;
5   et quotiens illam trepido cernebat amore,
                haerebat, tamquam vera Medusa foret.
           defuncta est tandem, haec iurgia ferre per umbras
                iamque ipsam mutam reddere Persephonem.

For *infanti aere* in line 4 cf. Hor. *Sat.* 2. 5. 40 'infantis statuas' and *Thes.*
I. 1073. 31. *haerebat* is sound, of course: whenever Catucia's husband
looked amorously at his beautiful wife he would stop in his tracks, as
though turned to stone. Note that with the last line in its original form the
first word, *Gorgoneos,* strikes the keynote to the entire poem.

340 (Luxorius)
De causidico turpi, qui concubam suam Charitem vocabat

           Esset causidici si par facundia nervo,
                impleret cuncti viscera negotii.
      .   *at* tamen invigilat *causis,* quae crimina pandunt:
                cum Veneris famula iure Priapus agit.

3 at *sched. Divion.:* ut *A*   4 cum V. famula *Klapp:* dum u. fabulā *A:* dum V.
tabulas *Baehrens*   famulum *Burman*

In line 3 read *et tamen.* Also I suspect that *causis* should be *cartis*; cf.
Augustin. *Contra Fel.* 2 'nullus litigator potuit sine suis chartis litigare'.
   The last line in Riese's text makes perfect sense *per se*: a Priapus like this
lawyer is entitled to have dealings with a handmaid of Venus (Charis); and
no doubt R.T. Bruère (*CPh* 57 (1962) 179) was right in detecting a play on
words: *iure agit cum* could mean 'goes to law with'. But nothing links line 3
with line 4. Two verses must have fallen out, containing the woman's
name, Charis or Charite, and accounting for the statement in the title that
the name had been given by her lover. As thus: 'invigilatque suae non
minus et Chariti. / huic nullum potuit tamen aptius indere nomen: / cum'
sqq.

343 (Luxorius)

In eum qui, cum senior dici nollet, multas sibi concubas faciebat et . . .

5   incassum reparare putas hac fraude iuventam;
          harum luxus agit, sis gravis ut senior.

      6 ut *L. Mueller:* aut *A*   senio *Baehrens*

senior was misunderstood by Riese: 'i.e. *dominus*'. The point is in a *double entendre. gravis,* 'grave', is what an old man should be, but this one is *gravis* in another sense. His affairs with mistresses do not make him any less of an old man, they only make him a *boring* old man. Cicero seems t make a similar jest in *Att.* 5. 12.2, 'Helonius' ('Helenius'? See *Two studies in Roman nomenclature* (1976) 43), 'homo gravissimus'.

345 (Luxorius)
Epitaphion de filia Oageis infantula

11   linguaque diversum fundebat mellea murmur,
          tamquam avium *verna resonat* per tempora cantus.

     12 verna resonat (resonet *Klapp*) *Riese:* uernaresolet *A:* verna ire solet *Baehrens*

Perhaps 'verni (= veris) resonet'.

354 (Luxorius)
In epitaphion supra scripti Olympii

Venator iucunde nimis atque arte ferarum
saepe *placens,* agilis gratus fortissimus audax...

      1 arti *A:* apte *L. Mueller*

A hunter's skill in the arena can hardly be called *ars ferarum.* Perhaps *placens* should be *potens.*

    The string of complimentary epithets is followed by a relative clause (34) which ends in Riese's text with a full stop. Cf. *AJPh* 97 (1976) 257: 'The tendency of Ausonius' editors to leave vocatives in the air can only be deplored' (also ibid. 252 and, on Paulin. Nol. *Carm.* 4.6 ff., ibid. 4). In this piece commas instead of full stops are in order at the ends of lines 4, 6, and 8.

361 (Luxorius)
In psaltriam foedam

Cum saltas misero, Gattula, corpore
nec cuiquam libitum est, horrida, quod facis,
insanam potius te probo psaltriam,
quae foedam faciem motibus *ingraves*

5   et, dum displiceas, quosque *feras* iocos.
       credis, quod populos cymbala mulceant?
       nemo iudicium tale animi gerit,
       pro te ut non etiam gaudia deserat.

2 libitum *Burman*: libido *A*	3 probo] puto *Maehly*	4 ingraves *Riese*
(?): ingrabas *A*: ingravas *vulg. olim*	8 non] nota *Baehrens*	deserat *vulg.*:
deserant *A*		

In line 3 the poet intimates that when he sees 'Kitty' dancing, at which
she is an unsightly failure, he admires her performance on the lute, which
she does well, or at least less badly. If *insanam* is right, translate: 'I approve
you, crazy as you are, rather as a lute-player'. But the adjective lacks point,
and I wonder whether we should not read *insanum* or *insane,* adverb with
probo; cf. the Plautine 'insanum bene' and Hofmann, *Lat.
Umgangssprache*[3] 78.

Lines 4-5 describe what happens when she dances. Indicatives, not
subjunctives, are required, so *ingravas* must be restored in 4. *feras* in 5 is
not only the wrong mood but the wrong sense. Read *patras*: 'and, as long as
you disgust the audience, you perpetrate all kinds of antics.' It is as though
she will do anything to annoy the public; whereas, of course, she herself
thinks in terms of doing anything to please it.

In the last two lines *iudicium animi* means 'critical taste' and *gaudia,* as
Riese explains, refers to the cymbals. 'nemo tale iudicium gerit ut non
deserat' = 'omnes tale iudicium gerunt ut deserant.' Everyone has taste
enough to forego the cymbals in order to get away from such dancing.
Riese explains *pro te* 'i.e. apud te, te visa'. Rather 'for your sake', with a
double meaning. On the face of it line 8 would mean: 'not to forsake even
pleasures for your sake (i.e. to see you)'; but in this context 'for your sake'
means 'to stop you making such an exhibition'.

363 (Luxorius)
In ebriosam et satis meientem

Quod bibis et totum *dimittis* ab inguine Bacchum,
    pars tibi superior debuit esse femur.
potabis recto (poteris, Follonia!) *Baccho,*
    si parte horridius inferiore bibas.

1 et *sched. Divion.: om. A*	demittis *Burman, recte, ut vid.*	3 potabis *Riese*:
potaris *A*: potare est *Burman*: potari *Meyer*		

As pointed out by Bruère in his review of Rosenblum (*CPh* 57 (1962)
179), the first couplet alludes to 'Bacchus' incubation in Jupiter's thigh'.
Follonia should drink from her thigh instead of her mouth. But *recto
Baccho* cannot mean 'with Bacchus in the proper place', and even if it could

the line cannot be as Luxorius wrote it. *Baccho* seems to be a reflexion from line 1 which has replaced a word with a meaning. I suggest 'potare et recto poteris, Follonia, vultu'; 'also you will be able to tipple with a straight face if you do your ungraceful drinking with the lower part.' It is implied that she drinks in an ugly fashion; if she does it with her thigh, her face will not have to be distorted.

364 (Luxorius)
In mulierem pulcram castitati studentem

5   te neque coniugii libet excepisse levamen,
      saepius *exoptas* nolle videre mares.
   haec tamen est animo quamvis exosa voluptas:
      numquid non mulier conparis esse potes?

5 iuvat...ligamen *Baehrens*   6 exoptas *Burman*: exoptans *AS*   8 con
paris *A*: cum paris *S*

Line 6 is unsatisfactory in two ways: the absence of a connective and the phrase *exoptas nolle,* which has to be regarded as a conflation of *exoptas non* and *dicis te nolle.* Both scruples are removed by substituting *et iactas* for *exoptas.* For the simple infinitive with *iactare* see *Thes.* VII. 1. 60. 46 (Statius and Claudian).

The last line is deliberately ambiguous. *conparis,* 'of someone like yourself', might mean a man as chaste as this lady is or pretends to be. It might also mean a woman who, like herself, is not interested in relations with the other sex.

365 (Luxorius)
De eo uui cum Burdo diceretur filiae suae Passiphaae nomen inposuit

   Disciplinarum esse hominem risusque capacem,
      quod nulli est pecudi, dixit Aristoteles.
   sed <cum> Burdo homo sit, versum est sophismate verum:
      nam et ridere solet *vel* ratione viget.
5   surrexit duplex nostro sub tempore monstrum,
      quod pater est burdo Passiphaeque redit.

3 cum *add. Salmasius*: si *Baehrens*   4 vel] et *Meyer*: nec *Baehrens*

Aristotle's truth has become fallacy. Since Burdo (Mule) is a man, he contradicts it in both parts: first, in that being a mule he laughs; second, in that being a man he lacks reason. The third couplet introduces a different point. Burdo is a father, which fact involves a twofold monstrosity: first, a mule has progeny; second, a woman has born a child to a beast. Whoever wrote the title misunderstood the last words. Pasiphae lives again as Burdo's wife, not as his daughter, and Pasiphae is not her name.

366 (Luxorius)
De laude rosae centumfoliae

Hanc puto de proprio tinxit Sol aureus ortu
  aut unum ex radiis maluit esse suis.
sed si *etiam centum* foliis rosa Cypridis extat,
  fluxit in hanc omni sanguine tota Venus.

3 sed] vel *Baehrens*   *etiam centu A: centum etiam *sched. Divion.*   4 hanc
Meyer: hac *A*   omni *Boissonade*: omnis *A*

Line 2 means: 'or he wished one of his rays rather to be this (rose)', i.e.
the rose was originally a ray of sunshine. If, however (*sed* is sound), this
rose of a hundred petals is, like other roses, a flower of Venus (and not after
all a product of the sun), then Venus has poured all her blood into it.
Perhaps read 'sed si centum cum foliis' (*cum* falls out after *centum* and
etiam is added *metri causa*).

367 (Luxorius)
De statua Hectoris in Ilio, quae videt Achillem et sudat

5   nescio quid *mirum gesserunt* Tartara *saeclo*:
    credo quod aut *superi* animas post funera reddunt
    aut ars mira potest legem mutare barathri.

5 cesserunt *Klapp*   saeclo *Salmasius*: sello *A*: caelo *Klapp*   6 superi (*sed
post* animas) *L. Mueller*: superis *A*: statuis *coni. Baehrens*

In line 5 Klapp's corrections should be accepted, but read: 'nescio quid
mirum <est>: cesserunt Tartara caelo'. In line 6 read *superis animas* (A), as
Baehrens does. Either, so it seems, Tartarus (i.e. the underworld)
voluntarily returns souls to the upper world after burial or great art can
change the underworld's rules.

371 (Luxorius)
De rustica in disco facta, quae spinam tollit de planta Satyri

Cauta nimis spinam Satyri pede rustica tollit,
  luminibus certis vulneris alta notans.
illam panduri solatur voce Cupido,
  inridens, *parili teste carere* virum.

3 illam pandurii (*sic*) solatur *Burman*: illum pandorii soletur *A*   4 parili
Burman: pariete *A*   carere *Burman*: gemēre *A*: dolere *Froehner*   pariter (*hoc iam
alii*) triste gemere *Tandoi*

Tandoi's elaborate discussion (*RFIC* 92 (1964) 397-421) cannot be
considered to have solved the textual problem in line 4. Perhaps read:

'inridens tali teste gemere virum' (or 'gemente viro'). Cupid laughs at the Satyr for making such a fuss in front of a girl. *parieteteste* may have arisen from a dittography *taliteteste.*

375 (Luxorius)
De catto qui, cum soricem maiorem devorasset, apoplexiam passus occubuit

3   pertulit adsuetae damnum per viscera praedae;
    per vitam moriens concipit ore necem.

Is *vitam* to be understood as *victum,* a use for which there seems to be no warrant after Plautus? *pro vita* would be easier. Or *et vivam*?

376 (Florentinus)
In laudem regis

5   in quo concordant pietas prudentia mores
   virtus forma decus animus *sensusque* virilis
   invigilans animo sollers super omnia †sensus.

7 mens est coni. Riese

sensus being evidently corrupt either in line 6 or in line 7, Riese made the wrong choice. Read in the former 'cultusque virilis', for which expression cf. Hor. *Od.* 1. 18. 15 and other passages cited by Gudeman on Tac. *Dial.* 26. 3. *virilis* qualifies both *animus* and *cultus.*

378 (Calbulus Grammaticus)
Versus fontis

11   marmoris oblati speciem, nova munera, supplex
   Calbulus exhibuit. fontis memor, unde renatus,
   per formam cervi gremium perduxit aquarum.

13 per Ziehen: et A

There should be no stop after *exhibuit* (Baehrens has none), or at most a comma; and the comma after *renatus* should disappear. 'fontis . . . aquarum' is interpreted from *Psalms* 41. 2 'quemadmodum desiderat cervus ad fontes aquarum, ita desiderat anima mea ad te, Deus': 'mindful of the spring from which, reborn, he drank the bosom of waters (i.e. God) after the manner of a stag'. But usage demands, not *per formam,* but *ad formam*; see *Thes.* VI. 1087.

383
De alcyonibus

Stat domus exerrans *constructa lymphis* et ulva.

fervet amor lymphis, liquescunt ova tepore.

1 construxit *Baehrens*   limfis *A*: limus *Baehrens*

'quam struxit limus'?

388a
\<Celeuma\>

10   aequora prora secet delphinis aemula saltu
      atque gemat largum, promat *seseque* lacertis,
      pone trahens canum deducat \<et\> orbita sulcum.

11 etque gemet *B*   12 et *add. Baehrens*

Perhaps 'promat se quisque lacertis / pone trahens, canum' *sqq.* The rowers, pulling backward at each stroke, force themselves and the boat forward through the water. Garrod's *Oxford book of Latin verse* (no. 307) has *se quisque*, presumably on his own conjecture.

389
In laudem solis

39   Sol cui *vernanti* tellus respirat odorem

uernanti *L*: uernantur *B*: vernantem *Opitius*: verna novum *Heinsius*

vernantem, read by Riese in his first edition but not mentioned in his second, seems to be right: cf. Drac. *Rom.* 10. 115 'vernalis odor'.

404 (Seneca?)
Item (i.e. epitaphion Pompeiorum, vel potius Pompeii)

Maxima civilis belli iactura † sub *ipso est*
      quantus quam parvo vix tegeris tumulo!

1 sed ipse es *Peiper*: sub ipso *Housman*   *lacunam inter duos versus stat. Baehrens*

Manilius says of Marius (4. 46): 'quod consul totiens, exul, quod \<de\> exule consul / adiacuit Libycis compar iactura ruinis', on which Housman cites Barth's observation that *iactura* there is equivalent to *ruina* and continues: 'In Anth. Lat. Riese 404, ubi tollendum *est,* praeterea nihil mutandum, Pompeius dicitur "maxima civilis belli iactura sub ipso", hoc est ruina magnitudine proxima ipsi bello civili omnes ruinas complexo'. More precisely, however, *iactura* in the Manilian line is 'what lies on the ground' ('a iacendo' Barth). With reference to a war such a use seems open to question. On the other hand *iactura* is often used of losses in war (*Thes.* VII. 2. 63. 59). Perhaps then we ought to consider:

Maxima civilis belli iactura sub isto es
      (quantus quam parvo vix tegeris!) tumulo.

405 (Seneca?)

Ad amicum optimum

5   solus honor nobis, arx et tutissima *nobis*...

The repetition of the pronoun in emphatic position lays a stress which it will hardly bear; contrast e.g. Catull. 63.65 'mihi ianuae frequentes, mihi limina tepida, / mihi floridis corollis redimita domus erat'. Perhaps read *nostris* at the end of the line.

412 (Seneca?)

In eum qui maligne iocatur

13   bellus homo es? *valide* capitalia crimina ludis
            deque tuis manant atra venena iocis!

> 13 es *Vonck*: et *V*   valde *coni. Baehrens*

Read 'bellus homo es? valde. capitalia' *sqq.* Cf. Plaut. *Pseud.* 344 'CAL. meam tu amicam vendidisti? BAL. valde, viginti minis.' The form *valide* = *valde* is found only in Plautus.

413 (Seneca?)

De insepultis claris

Litore diverso Libyae clarissima longe
    nomina vix ullo condita sunt tumulo,
Magnus et *hoc* Magno maior Cato.

> 3 hoc Magno *Scaliger, qui tamen* humano *edidit*: hoc homine *V*: ob finem *Baehrens*

Riese, who claims *hoc Magno* as his own conjecture, compares Ov. *Ex Pont.* 4. 3. 41 'quid fuerat Magno maius', which, however, says nothing for *hoc.* Read *hinc Magno. hinc* = *alia parte*; cf. *Thes.* VI. 2805. 80.

415 (Seneca?)

De spe

13   saepe bono rursusque malo blandissima *saepe* <*est*>;
            et quos decepit, decipit illa tamen.

> 13 saepe est *Riese*: semp(er) *V*: serpit *Russo*   semperque m. b. rursus *Baehrens*

Read: 'saepe bono, rursusque malo, blandissima semper, / et quos' *sqq.* The text of the Vossianus needs explanation, not emendation; but the explanation in Barth's *Adversaria* (XXIII. 12), which satisfied Burman, is wrong. *bono* and *malo* are predicative datives; cf. Phaedr. 5.4.12 'paucis temeritas est bono, multis malo'. *et* in line 14 = *etiam*.

418 (Seneca?)

Item (i.e. memoriam litteris permanere)

3   tu licet extollas magnos ad sidera montes
         et *calidas* aeques marmore pyramidas.

   4 Pharias *Heinsius*: validas *Pithoeus* (?): solidas *Pierson*: canas *Baehrens*

Riese explains *calidas* 'i.e. in Africa sitas' and ignores *solidas* and *validas.*
The first merits consideration; cf. 443.1 'quod tua mille domus solidas
habet alta columnas'. But the pyramids are *not* solid, and Seneca (if he is
really the author) had lived in Egypt and would probably have known this.
So *validas,* ignored also by Baehrens, seems preferable; cf. Lucr. 5. 1440
'validis saepti degebant turribus aevum'. Here the force has to be 'strong
against the assaults of time'.

421
<Item> (i.e. Laus Caesaris)

Euphrates ortus, Rhenus *secluserat* Arctos:
   Oceanus medium venit in imperium.

   1 secluserat *Cannegieter*: recl- *V*: praecl- *Baehrens*

The meaning is: now that the Ocean is part of the Empire (after the
conquest of Britain) the former barriers to the north and east will cease to
operate; cf. 425. 1 'opponis frustra rapidum, Germania, Rhenum; /
Euphrates prodest nil tibi, Parthe fugax; / Oceanus iam terga dedit, nec
pervius ulli / Caesareos fasces imperiumque tulit' and Sen. *Suas.* 4. 3
'Babylon ei cluditur cui patuit Oceanus?' Read *recluserit* (= *recludet*; cf.
K.-S. I. 147 ff.). Cf. also Philo, *Leg. ad Gaium* 10.

426 (Seneca?)
<Item> (i.e. Laus Caesaris)

3   quam (*sc.* Britanniam) pater invictis Nereus *velaverat* undis

        qua *V*   vallaverat *Scaliger*: celaverat *Baehrens*

vallaverat is clearly right. The idea of Britain surrounded by natural
ramparts occurs in Cic. *Att.* 4. 16. 7 'constat enim aditus insulae esse
muratos mirificis molibus', though that doubtless refers to the cliffs of
Dover. Professor C.P. Jones compares Shakespeare, *Richard II,* Act 2, sc. 1
'this fortress built by Nature for herself'.

435 (Seneca?)
<De ea quae amat>

Quaedam me (si credis) amat. sed dissilit, ardet
   non sic, non leviter, sed perit et moritur.

dum faciet gratis quaedam, simul atque rogaro,
      ostendam, quam non semper amatus amem.

3 faciet *Riese*: figiet *V*: fugiet *V corr.*: fugio et *Prato*   dum gratis, flagret
Baehrens   rogaro *Riese, qui etiam* rogavi *coni.*: rogauit *V*: rogabit *Scaliger*

Read 'ni faciet'.

440 (Seneca?)
De bono quietae vitae

3   ante nives calidos demittent *fontibus* amnes
        et Rhodanus *nullas* in mare ducet aquas...

In line 3 read *montibus*; cf. *Dirae* 13 'ipsae non silvae frondes, non
flumina montes' (sc. 'parturiant'). *nullas . . . aquas* recalls Prop. 1. 15. 29 in
Barber's text: 'nulla' (*multa* codd.) 'prius vasto labentur flumina ponto',
where *nulla* is unsatisfactory because it 'gives no positive inversion of
nature's laws' (Butler-Barber). To the dozen or so conjectures in Smyth's
Thesaurus criticus ad Sexti Propertii textum might be added *salsa*; and here
salsas . . . aquas would balance *nives calidos* well enough; cf. *Herc. Oet.*
1582 'ante nascetur seges in profundo / vel fretum dulci resonabit unda'.

445 (Seneca?)
De amico mortuo

Ablatus mihi Crispus est, *amici*...

amici *vulg.*: amihi *V*: amicus *Baehrens*

The address *amici* is suspect, even though not so demonstrably wrong as
in Hor. *Epod.* 13.3 (see Housman, *Classical papers* 1087). Nor does it seem
likely that the poem was addressed to an unknown Amicius (see ibid.).
When occasionally a poem in this group is addressed to an individual,
other than such as Homer or the Emperor, the names tend to be
commonplace, like Maximus, Crispus, Galla. Perhaps *inique*; cf. Sen. *Dial.*
6. 26. 2 'ut inique actum cum filio tuo iudices', Catull. 101. 6 'heu miser
indigne frater adempte mihi!', *Cons. Liv.* 187 'iniqua ad funera.' If so, and
assuming that *amihi* is a mere miswriting, we have an example of 'the old
and widespread confusion of "qu" and "c"' (Housman, ibid. 97).

450 (Seneca?)
De silentio amoris

Iuratum tibi me cogis promittere, Galla,
      ne narrem. iura rursus et ipsa mihi,
ne cui tu dicas – nimium est lex dura; remittam: –
      praeterquam si vis dicere, Galla, viro!

The second couplet needs a new punctuation: 'ne cui tu dicas. nimium
est lex dura? remittam, / praeterquam, si vis, dicere, Galla, viro': I will let
you tell, except, if you please, your husband'. For the infinitive with
remitto cf. Ov. *Met.* 11. 376 'nec res dubitare remittit'.

452 (Seneca?)

De tinnitu auris

'Garrula, quod totis resonant mihi noctibus aures,
    nescioquem *dicis* nunc meminisse mei?'
'hic quis sit, quaeris? resonant *tibi* noctibus aures,
    et resonant totis: Delia *te* loquitur'.
'non dubie loquitur me Delia: mollior aura
    venit et exili murmure dulce fremit.

   1 quod *V*: quid *Scaliger*   3 resonant *Riese*: resonas *V*

From line 5 on the supposed interlocutor vanishes. I do not believe he, or
she (*garrula*!), was ever there. *garrula* is neut. plur. (adverbial accusative
with *resonant*), and in what follows I would substitute 'dicas . . . mihi . . .
me' for 'dicis . . . tibi . . . te'. The first couplet should be a statement rather
than a question.

461 (Seneca?)

De Atho monte

9   quale fuit regnum, mundo nova ponere iura!
        'hoc terrae fiat, *hac* mare' dixit 'eat'.

   10 terrae *Scaliger*: terra *V*   hic terrae fiant *Toup*   hac *vulg.*: ac *V*   hoc
mare, dixit: erant *Gronovius*

Gronovius is to be followed (neither Baehrens nor Riese record that he
proposed *hoc*), except that there is no necessity for the plural *erant. erat* is
just as good.

462 (Seneca?)

De malo belli civilis

9   fratribus heu fratres, patribus concurrere natos
        impia sors belli fataque saeva iubent.
       hic generum, socerum ille petit, *minimeque* cruentus
        qui fuit, <is> sparsus sanguine civis erat.

   11 ille *Scaliger*: q. *V*: -ve *Oudendorp*   12 is sparsus *L. Mueller*: sparsus *V*:
adspersus *Heinsius, fort. recte*

Amid concern for the metre in line 4 the sense seems to have passed
unregarded. Whether a soldier kills a brother, an unknown fellow-

countryman, or a foreign enemy, he is equally *cruentus*. Nor will it do
to understand 'he who shed the least quantity of blood shed the blood of a
fellow-countryman'. That loses the connexion. The relevant comparison is
not between those who killed many adversaries (usually creditable in a
fighting man) and those who killed few, but between those who killed their
kin and those who merely killed fellow-Romans. Read *minimoque*. Many
killed close relatives, and those who shed blood at the smallest cost (in
guilt), i.e. who did not kill their kin, yet killed their countrymen.

464 (Petronius?)

Inveniat, quod quisque *velit.* non omnibus unum est,
    quod placet. hic spinas colligit, ille rosas.

1 inueniet *V*: inceptet *coni. Baehrens*   velit *ex* uelet *V m. 1*

Read 'inveniet quod quisque volet'. 'Two men looked through prison bars.
/ One saw mud, the other stars.' For the future *volet* cf. Cic. *Off.* 2. 43 'qui
igitur adipisci veram gloriam volet, iustitiae fungatur officiis' *et sim.* (K.-S.
I. 144f.).

465 (Petronius?)

Iam nunc ardentes autumnus fregerat *umbras...*

ardentes *vulg.*: argentes *V*: algentes *Baehrens*   fregerat *vulg.*: regerat *V*: fecerat
Baehrens

Read 'ardentes . . . fregerat horas' with Housman on Manil. 4. 341. His
illustrations can now be supplemented from *Thes.* VI. 2964.

466 (Petronius?)

12   et voti reus, et qui *vendidit orbem,*
    iam sibi quisque deos avido certamine fingit.

12 furti *Baehrens*   orbum *Barth*: urbem *Pithoeus*

Gods were created by men to suit their several callings or occasions. The
poem presents a series of examples, these two being the last. If *voti reus* is
sound, as I believe it is, the expression is used loosely for *exoptatae rei
compos*. The man who obtained his wish invented a god to thank. *vendidit
orbem* is rubbish. Read *condidit urbem*; cf. Virg. *Aen.* 3. 19 'sacra Dionaeae
matri divisque ferebam / auspicibus coeptorum operum'.

474 (Petronius?)

O litus vita mihi dulcius! o mare felix,
    cui licet ad terras ire subinde meas!

o formosa dies! hoc quondam *rure* solebam
†*Iliadas armatas* sollicitare *manus.*

2 meas] tuas *Baehrens*   3 dies] quies *Heinsius*   4 Iliadum *Pithoeus*:
Iliada *Christ*: Naidas *Lindenbrog*   armata s. manu *Christ*: alterna s. manu *Butler*

The poet's playmate(s) must remain anonymous. *Heliada* (cf. Dessau *Inscr. Lat.* 8098) may be added to the possibilities. But *rure* can be changed with confidence to *rore.* The poet used to splash his mistress(es) in the water. Nor have I much question about accepting 'alterna . . . manu' for which its author (*CR* 26 (1912) 221) compared Prop. 1. 11. 12 'alternae facilis cedere lympha manu'.

476 (Petronius?)

8   concepit nam terra sonos calamique loquentes
     invenere Midam, qualem narraverat index.

9 invenere Midam *Fulgentius, Myth. 3. 8*: inuenerem idem *V*: incinuere Midam *Salmasius*: insonuere Midam *Wernsdorf*

The wanted word is 'vulgavere'.

483 (Sisebutus)
Regis Gothorum epistula missa ad Isidorum de libro rotarum

7   et trans Oceanum ferimur porro usque nivosus
     cum *teneat* Vasco nec parcat Cantaber horrens.

Burman's note points out that line 8 echoes Venant. Fort. 10. 25 'Cantaber ut timeat, Vasco vagus arma pavescat'; but *teneat* makes no sense. Read *tumeat*; cf. Tac. *Hist.* 2. 32 'quoniam Galliae tumeant', Ov. *Her.* 7. 121 'bella tument'.

485 (Citherius rhetor)
De figuris vel schematibus
Διῃρημένον

58   †Disparsum reddo, quod passum non ordine reddo†
     'ambo Iovis merito proles, verum ille equitando
     insignis Castor, catus hic pugilamine Pollux'.

tit. Διῃρημένον *Quicherat*: Διερειμμένον *P*   1 passum] sparsum *Sauppe*   non] uno *Quicherat*

Read: 'dispersum reddo quod sparsum uno ordine iungo'. In the illustration the Twins are first combined, then separated.

'Επιτροπή

70   Fit concessio, cum quidvis concedimus optet.
        'nescivit vel non potuit vel noluit: ut vis,
        pone, tibi permitto; tamen non debuit *uti*'.

'ut vis, pone' = 'put it as you wish'. In 72 read 'non debuit ille' (*sc.* 'ita facere').

'Ισόκωλον

82   Fit parimembre, ubi membra †*aequa et circuitus* sunt.
            aequali circuitu *Baehrens*

Read 'aequato circuitu'.

Χαρακτηρισμός

148   Fit depictio, cum verbis ut imagine pingo.
        'pocula, serta tenens flexa cervice iacebat,
        limodes, gravis optutu, madido ore renidens'.

                150 limodes *Haase*: limonides *P*

Not *limodes* (λιμώδης), 'hungry', but *lemodes* (λημώδης), 'bleary'.

485a (Lactantius)
De ave phoenice

97   aetherioque procul de lumine concipit ignem:
            flagrat, et ambustum (*sc.* phoenicis corpus) solvitur in
                                                                    cineres.
        quos velut in massam, *generans in morte,* coactos
        conflat, et effectum seminis instar habet.

        98 cineres *Ritschl*: cinerem *codd.*   99 generans *Ziehen*: cineres *PL*: cineris *V*:
    natura *Ritschl*   in morte *codd. recc.*: in more *PVL*: umore *Ritschl*: *alii alia*

The subject in 99 f. has to be something moist; and the body of the phoenix reduced to ashes cannot be said *effectum seminis instar habere.* Read:

            et ambustum solvitur in cinerem.
        ros velut in massam cineres umore coactos
            conflat...

For the repetition 'cinerem . . . cineres' cf. 90 'vitalique toro membra vieta locat. / ore dehinc sucos membris circumque supraque / inicit'.

103   crescit, et emenso sopitur tempore certo,
            seque ovi teretis colligit in speciem.

        103 crescit et *Riese*: creuerit *PVL*: crescit in *codd. recc.*   emenso *Brandt*: immensum
    codd.   sopitur *Klapp*: subitus *P*: subito *L*: subitur *V, P corr.*

The subject is the worm (*vermis*) which developed from the moist ashes. Perhaps 'crescit et emenso' (or 'immensum' cf. Ov. *Fast.* 5. 537 'creverat immensum') 'sufflatur'.

139 arquatur cuncto capiti radiata corona,
   Phoebei referens verticis alta decus.

139 arquatur (*Klapp*) cuncto *Riese*: aequataque not(h)o *VL*: aptatur noto *Oudendorp*: *alii alia*

Perhaps 'aptaturque aucto'; cf. Val. Flac. 6. 532 'frontem . . . cornibus auxit'.

490 (Tiberianus)
Versus Platonis de Graeco in Latinum translati

13 scilicet ut mundo redeat, quod partubus †*austrum*
  perdiderit refluumque iterum *per tempora* fiat.

13 partubus *vulg.*: partibus *RP* austrum *R*: abstrum *P*: aethra *G. Hermann*: haustus *Baehrens* partibus (= e partibus) haustum *Quicherat* 14 tempora *R*: corpora *P*

Read 'partubus haustum'. The spirit returns to the universe from which it was drawn by births in mortal bodies; cf. Cic. *Divin.* 1. 70 'animos hominum quadam ex parte extrinsecus esse tractos et haustos', *Thes.* VI. 2568. 64. In the next line read 'post corpora', 'after leaving the bodies'. The contracted forms of *per* and *post* are readily confused.

32 quidque id sit vegetum, *quod per cita* corpora *vivit*

quidque id sit *Baehrens*: quidquid id est *RP* quod per cita *R*: per concita *P*

Read 'quo percita corpora vivunt'.

490a
Officia duodecim mensium
Artatur niveus bruma Ianuarius †arva.

atra *coni. Riese*: alba *Mariotti*

Before encountering Mariotti's conjecture (*ap.* S. Timpanaro, *SIFC* 25 (1951) 42) I had thought of *aspra*, a regular epithet of winter; cf. *Thes.* II. 809. 55. But *alba* has the advantage palaeographically. Its author compares Avien. *Arat.* 987 'albenti cum canent tempora bruma'. Add 'cana bruma' in Sen. *Phaedr.* 966 and Stat. *Theb.* 4. 832, also Mart. 1. 49. 19 'December canus et bruma impotens'.

5 Maius hinc gliscens herbis *generat*† *nigra bella.*

nigra vela (*i.e.* arborum umbras (!)) *Buecheler*: sola bella *Baehrens*

Perhaps 'creat arva novella'.

494b
Laus Herculis

2   Phoebe, precor, huc age, laeto...
    tecum †cuncta choro

2 laeto, precor, huc age, Phoebe *Cannegieter*   3 tecum] comple *Morel*   cuncta] iunge *Claverius*

Read 'huc age laeto / te comitante choro'. For *se agere* = *se movere* see *Thes.* I. 1372. 1.

58   *et manibus teneris* cogens in bracchia pondus
      constringis pressos, relevans tellure, dracones.

58 et *vulg.*: ex *V*   manibus *Riese*: quamuis *V*   teneris *Camers*: teneri *V*   59 sic *Riese*: corripis (*ex v. 57*) impressos liuens t. d. *V*: *alii alia*

'corporis et teneri'?

65   his coeptis non ulla parat cunabula *partus,*
    dive, tibi; sed cum *totis* iam bruma rigeret
    imbribus et solidis haererent flumina lymphis,
    nudum praegelidis durando firmat in undis.

66 diva (*i.e.* Alcmena) *Camers*

partus makes a strange subject for 'nudum firmat in undis'. It will have arisen from *parat,* displacing *virtus;* cf. 87 'at nullum virtus reticenda per aevum / ... posse mori quam vile putat!' and 113 (see below). 'his coeptis' is abl. abs. *partus* (*part'*) might also be replaced with *mater* (*mat'*) but *secura iam matre* in 70 is somewhat against that, suggesting, as it does, that Alcmena was a normally anxious parent.

totis in 66 can hardly be right. *effusis* vel sim. (*ruptis*? cf. Virg. *Aen.* 11. 548 'tantus se nubibus imber / ruperat') might have been expected. See above on 200. 60 (*ruptis* for *totis*).

108   sternebatque suis lugentia rura colonis

ingentia *coni. Riese olim*

The boar strewed the fields with the corpses of their farmers. For *lugentia* cf. Cic. *Verr.* 2. 3. 47 'ut ager ipse cultorem desiderare ac lugere dominum videretur', *Phil.* 10. 8 'o spectaculum illud non modo hominibus sed undis ipsis et litoribus luctuosum', Clark on *Mil.* 20, R.G.M. Nisbet on *Pis.* 21 'templa gemerent'.

113   nec vulnera virtus
    exemplo *tibi* facta timet.

Read *sibi,* as Wernsdorf would have liked to do. Hercules' valour is better conceived as having set an example to itself than to Hercules.

116   atque supinando mirantem *lumina vinci*
    Argolici victor portas sub tecta tyranni.

    116 lumina *Camers*: limina *V*   vinctum *Birt*

vinctum, favoured by Riese ('recte?'), fulfils what is almost mandatory in this context; for according to the common version of the legend followed in this poem Hercules brought the Erymanthian boar to Argos alive in bonds; cf. Apoll. Rhod. 1. 129 δεσμοῖς ἰλλόμενον, Philippson, *RE* VI. 566. But I fail to see any light in *lumina* for *limina* and propose *vimine* (λύγοις); cf. Calp. *Ecl.* 3. 71 'tradimus ecce manus; licet illae vimine torto / scilicet et lenta post tergum vite domentur'. The sequence of participles 'mirantem .. vinctum' is rather clumsy, and it might be better to write: 'mirantem vimine vinci<s> / Argolici <et> victor' *sqq.*

<h3 style="text-align:center">526 (Euphorbius)</h3>

    Forma *repercussus* liquidarum *fingit* aquarum,
    qualis purifico 'speculorum ex orbe relucet.

    1 repercussu . . . fertur *coni. Riese*

One of a series of twelve distichs, allegedly by different authors, on water and mirrors. Perhaps 'repercussu . . . surgit'.

<h3 style="text-align:center">642 (Q. Cicero)</h3>

8   autumni reserat portas aequatque diurna
    tempora nocturnis *dispenso* sidere Libra.

suspenso, 'poised', would make better sense. *dispenso* is interpreted in the Thesaurus as 'i. q. quasi aequa lance perpendere', but no parallel quoted.

<h3 style="text-align:center">649 (Servasius)</h3>
<h4 style="text-align:center">De cupiditate</h4>

23   mirum ni pulcras artes Romana iuventus
      discat et egregio sudet in eloquio,
    ut post iurisonae *famosa* stipendia linguae
      barbaricae ingeniis anteferantur opes?

    25 iurgisonae clamosa impendia *Heinsius*

Not a question but an ironical statement (so Vinetus *ap.* Burman): 'It would be strange if they didn't learn' = 'No wonder they don't learn'; cf. *Thes.* VIII. 1074. 30. *famosă stǐpendia* should not be tolerated in a poem of 42 lines which otherwise conforms to classical prosody; even in late antiquity a short vowel before *st* et sim. is very rare. Possibly *famosa* should be *frustra*, used adjectivally.

653 (Sulpicius Carthaginiensis)
Hexasticha in Aeneidis libris

14   . . . ac tum dolus introducitur hostis
et fallacis equi damnosum munus, inermis
perfidia *notusque* Sinon.

The right reading is clearly *ignotusque*; cf. *Aen.* 2. 59 'qui se ignotum venientibus ultro, / hoc ipsum ut strueret Troiamque aperiret Achivis, / obtulerat', Quint. Smyrn. 12.33 τόν γ' οὕτις ἐπίσταται ἐν Τρώεσσι, 238 ὃν ὃν σάφα Τρῶες ἴσασι. *perfidia* belongs to *inermis*; Sinon's defenceless state was part of his strategem.

26   *clausum* †*veneratur amorem*
dumque capit, capitur: sentit, *quos* praebuit *ignes.*

26 venatur *Burman*   clauso venatur amore *Ribbeck*

Ribbeck may be followed (with Baehrens) in 26. What kan be made of 'praebuit ignes' in the next line? The words should take up the point, 'dumque capit, capitur' (cf. 654. 18 'capitur venatibus ipsa'). Perhaps 'quas . . . artes (venandi)'.

29   extructa regina pyra penetralibus instat
morte fugam †*praestare morae* nec defuit *hora.*

Read 'morte fugam pensare (Baehrens) viri (coni. Riese), nec defuit Iris'; cf. 34 'quibus additur Iris', 56 'Iris adest'.

672 ('Octavianus Caesar Augustus')

35   huc huc, Pierides, date flumina cuncta, sorores;
exspirent ignes, vivat Maro *ductus* ubique.

36 ductus *PB*: doctus *V*: cultus *coni. Riese*

Read *lectus. docenda* has been proposed for *legenda* in Avian. *Fab.* praef. (*HSPh* 82 (1978 295).

694 (Petronius)

7   lex armata sedet circum fera limina nuptae;
nil *metuit* licito fusa puella toro.

The theme of the poem is that a kindly deity ('candidus deus') has placed within easy reach the means to satisfy man's needs – food, drink, warmth, (as pointed out by R.T. Clark, *CR* 27 (1915) 92 f., *rogus* should not be changed to *focus* in line 6), and sex. As to the last, men who have affairs with married women risk punishment; but if you are content with what is permitted (and readily available), you will come to no harm. Horace (*Sat.* 1. 2. 115) teaches the same lesson: 'num esuriens fastidis omnia praeter /

pavonem rhombumque? tument tibi cum inguina, num, si / ancilla aut verna est praesto puer, impetus in quem / continuo fiat, malis tentigine rumpi? / non ego; namque parabilem amo Venerem facilemque'.

metuit must be taken to mean 'a girl has nothing to fear, and so neither has her lover'. But there is no purpose in the circumlocution. Read *nocuit*.

696 (Petronius)

Iudaeus licet et porcinum numen adoret
et caeli summas advocet auriculas,
ni tamen et ferro succiderit inguinis oram
et nisi nodatum solverit arte caput,
5   exemptus populo *Graia* migrabit *ab urbe*
et non ieiuna sabbata lege *premet*.

5 grata *Casaubon*: sacra *coni. Baehrens*   Graias m. ad urbes *Binet*: Graiam m. ad urbem *Goldastiana*

The piece probably comes from the *Satyricon*. I concern myself here only with the last couplet.

However conscientiously a Jew observes his religion in other ways, unless he is circumcised he must leave the community. In line 5 'Graiam migrabit ad urbem' is an easy change, whether it means 'to a Greek town' or 'to the Greek part of town' (hardly = *Romam*; cf. Riese: '*Graia* ad Euandrum Arcadem Palatii incolam spectare videtur'). Haseltine's translation of line 6, 'he will not transgress the Sabbath by breaking the law of fasting' is not in the Latin and means nothing relevant. Read 'at nos . . . prement'. The speaker was presumably an orthodox Jew.

700 (Petronius)

6   sed sic sic sine fine feriati
et tecum iaceamus osculantes.

7 tecum] sectim *Loewe* (*!*)   tractim *Baehrens*

Can we construe 'feriati et osculantes tecum iaceamus'? Cf. K.-S. I. 28, *Thes.* IV. 1377. 71, including Auson. *Parent.* 30. 11 'annua . . . ferimus . . . tibi iusta . . . / cum genero et natis consocer Ausonius'. Without *ego* it hardly seems possible. Perhaps *tu mecum*?

714 (Alcimus)

O blandos·oculos et †infacetos
et quadam propria nota loquaces!

1 et inquietos *Binet*: nec inquietos *Buecheler*: et o facetos *Baehrens*: et infaceto *F. Walter*   2 et] sed *Buecheler*

Perhaps 'item facetos'.

719b (Tiberianus)
Versus Socrati philosophi

23   aurum, *res* gladii, furor amens, ardor avarus...

res] lis *Baehrens*: cos *Rossberg*

cos is highly ingenious, but I fancy the answer is *spes.* Cicero's MSS have
rem for *spem* in *Rosc. Com.* 29.

725

28   dignus utroque stetit <deus> ostro clarus et auro...

deus *add. Peiper*: dux *Baehrens*

That *deus* was in the original is not certain, but if it was it came before
stetit, not after.

726 (Carmen Einsidlense II)

28   *nullo* iam noxia *partu*
          femina *quaecumque* est hostem parit.

'partu . . . parit' is inelegant and 'quaecumque est' pointless. Read
'nullum . . . parte . . . quacumque est'; cf. Hor. *Od.* 3. 3. 38 'qualibet exsules
/ in parte regnanto beati', 55 'qua parte debacchentur ignes'.

728
Versus ad puellam

7   exultent nostro *magnae* certamine nymphae,
                    tactibus exultes tuque puella meis!

The nymphs may have come from Virg. *Aen.* 4. 168 'summoque
ululaverunt vertice nymphae', but why *magnae? laetae?*

747
De cereo

          Flora venit. quae Flora? dea an de gente Latina?
                    non reor; *at* Chloris dicta per arva fuit.

2 at] et *Baehrens*

The first line runs: ' "Flora venit". "quae Flora?" "dea". "an de gente
Latina?" ' In the pentameter (cf. Ov. *Fast.* 5. 195) *at* is clearly wrong, but
neither does *et* seem to have any legitimate business. Perhaps *haec.*

760a (Eleg. in Maecenatem I)

57   Bacche, coloratos, postquam devicimus Indos,
                    potasti galea dulce iuvante merum.

et tibi securo tunicae fluxere solutae:
te puto purpureas tunc habuisse *duas*.

'Non intellego' Riese. The Duffs, guided by earlier wisdom, understood; 'to wear two was a sign of luxury'. Read *genas* (cf. *Thes.* VI. 1768. 43). On Bacchus' οἰνωπαὶ παρειαί see Dodds on Eur. *Bacch.* 236. *ge* may have dropped out after *se* leaving *habuissenas*.

93   sic est: victor amet, victor *potiatur* in umbra,
            victor odorata dormiat inque rosa.

93 spatietur *Scaliger*

J. Diggle (*Maia* 4 (1972) 347f.) defends the Latinity of 'potiatur' (sc. *eo quod amat*) and regards the couplet as presenting three aspects of the same experience; 'for the man who sleeps on scented roses does not always sleep alone.' But the third aspect is insufficiently distinguished from the second, and surely wine would not be left out; cf. Sall. *Cat.* 11.6 'ibi primum insuevit exercitus populi Romani amare potare'. For 'potiat'' I would read 'iāpotet (iam potet)'.

103   Caesar amicus erat; poterat vixisse solute,
            cum iam Caesar idem *quod* cupiebat erat.

The Duffs' rendering, 'so he was free to live a life of ease when the Emperor was now all he longed to be', has no logical connexion with 'Caesar amicus erat'; and *idem* does not mean 'all'. The poet is arguing from the commonplace that friends desire the same things; cf. e.g. Cic. *Planc.* 5 'vetus est enim lex illa iustae veraeque amicitiae . . . ut idem amici semper velint', *Cluent.* 46 'iam hoc fere scitis omnes quantam vim habeat ad coniungendas amicitias studiorum ac naturae similitudo'. Since Caesar was Maecenas' friend, it followed that Caesar must share his tastes, *cupere idem,* which meant that Maecenas could indulge them without apology. *quod* is translatable ('idem iam erat (id) quod Caesar cupiebat'), but I prefer *qui* ('iam Caesar erat qui idem cupiebat').

806
(Argumenta Lucani)

13   hinc pars quarta notat Pompeium tunc properasse
            Brundisium; tandemque videns maris ostia claudi
            Hesperiam puppesque duas in *parte* reliquit.

15 parte *Buecheler*: mare *E*: morte *T*

What *in parte* may have conveyed to Bücheler and the editors who followed him I have not sought to discover, but the word behind *mare* and *morte* is *mole*. The two unlucky Pompeian ships stuck fast in the narrow channel left by Caesar's mole between the harbour of Brundisium and the

open sea (Luc. 2. 709 ff.); so Caes. *B. C.* 1. 28. 4 'duasque... naves... quae
ad moles Caesaris adhaeserant, scaphis lintribusque reprehendunt'.

23   at quarti libri narrat pars prima, quod ivit
         Caesar *in* Hispanos *ad* iussa ducesque reversos.

24 in Barth: ad ET

Read 'Caesar ad Hispanos et' (*sc.* narrat) 'iussa'. 'Orders and generals
reversed' refers to the final submission of Afranius and Petreius; cf. Luc. 4.
337 'iam domiti cessere duces, pacisque petendae / auctor damnatis
supplex Afranius armis / semianimas in castra trahens hostilia turmas /
victoris stetit ante pedes'.

808

Aegritudo Perdicae

72   heu, Perdica, gravis aestus radiosque micantes
         solis te fugisse putas *lucosque* petisse

. . . .

         ignoras: intus gravior tibi flamma paratur!

Tired with hunting, Perdica enters a grove (63a). He thinks he has
escaped the heat, little knowing that he will there contract the fever of love.

Baehrens remarked that *lucosque* needs an epithet such as *igne vacuos.*
This of course could make up part of the gap which editors assume after 73.
73. But it is far more likely that *lucos* is an interpolation, introduced to fill
the line after *putas p(o)enasque* had been reduced to *putasque.* After the
lengthy description of the grove beginning in 25 ('lucus erat') and the
statement of Perdica's arrival in 63 ('ad lucum Perdica venit'), not to
mention the graphical similarity to *putas, lucos* would be the first word to
suggest itself. Thus the hypothesis of a lacuna in the text becomes
unnecessary.

121   des requiem miserando precor, et posse fateri.
122   'at matri *narrabo* nefas'. tamen ibo coactus?
124   'credamus?' quibus hoc poteris conponere verbis
125   aut vox qualis erit? *adgressus* namque parentem
123   'mater, ave' dicturus ero. quid deinde? tacebo!
126   Oedipodem thalamos matris vult fama subisse
         incestosque toros: satis est *quod* nescius *iste*
         commisit, culpamque tulit licet ille nefandam,
         exegit, sese *privat dum* lumine, poenam.

  122 at *Ellis*: et *H*   127 iste *Hiller*: ista *H*   128 ille *vulg.*: illi
H   129 privat dum *vulg.*: priuato *H*

Perdica's appeal to Cupid (121) to let him confess his incestuous love is
answered by his other self: 'But to tell your mother' (read *narrare*) 'is an

abomination'. The ensuing brief dialogue between, let us call them, P and
Π has been reduced to a shambles by Riese's reshuffling of the verses. This
is how it proceeds:

122   'at matri narrare nefas'. 'tamen ibo coactus.
         "mater, ave" dicturus ero.' 'quid deinde?' 'tacebo'.
         'credamus. quibus hoc poteris' *sqq.*

P. All the same, I shall go perforce. I shall say 'Hallo, mother.'
Π. And what then?
P. I shall hold my tongue.
Π. We had better believe it! How will you be able to put such a thing
into words, what sort of language will you use?
The second self continues:

125   adgressum namque parentem
         Oedipodem thalamos matris vult fama subisse
         incestosque toros. satis est. sed nescius ista
         commisit, *sqq.*

'Indeed the story goes that Oedipus attacked his father and married his
mother. That's bad enough. But he did it all in ignorance and, dreadful as
his guilt was, he punished himself for it'. *parentem = Laium,* and this can
join the passages quoted in *Propertiana* 103 on Prop. 2. 20. 15 'ossa tibi iuro
per matris et ossa parentis'. In 127 *quod* must become *sed,* but the change of
ista to *iste* (with *ille* to follow) is merely detrimental. In 128 'privat dum' is
one of several possibilities, and not the most likely: 'privat cum (c̄),
privando, exigit <a> sese'.

138   famulosque vocavit
         ad sese *iussitque artis medicae <venerandos>*
         primores qui forte forent, adducere secum.
         139 *sic Riese:* artis medicinae requiri *H*

Line 139 in H seems to be a botch. The original cannot be restored with
assurance, but may have run: 'ad sese, iussit medicinae protinus artis'.

160   *stridenti gremio* vivaces inpedit auras.

'Non intellegitur' Riese. Doctor Hippocrates is reeling off a series of
symptoms which the patient does *not* have (156-164). Every item is
introduced with a negative, *non.* It is therefore a safe assumption that line
160, which must originally have stated that there was nothing wrong with
Perdica's respiration, began in the same way. The remaining step is to
emend *stridenti gremio,* which arose *metri causa* after *non* had fallen out:
'non stridens gremium vivaces impedit auras'.

226   hoc visum placitum matri. non distulit ultra.

non] nec Baehrens

Read: 'hoc visum matri; placitum non distulit ultra'.

234   has tristis Perdica videns et lumina flectens
           in matrem traxit †dura suspiria corde
           et tali secum miser est sermone locutus.
           'pro dolor, o superi! defecerat altera forma:
           mater amanda fuit. sed vincere certo furorem
           quaerendo vultus, liceat quos iure tenere.
           hoc etiam voluisse nefas...'

   235 dura] dubio *Rossberg*: duram *Baehrens*   238 certo *Riese*: certas
H   furorem *coni. Baehrens* (-res *in text.*): furore *H*

dura in 235 seems to be another stopgap. Similar expressions suggest that *penitus* (*penit'*) fell out after *traxit*; cf. Dracont. *Orest.* 581 'suspiria traxit ab imo / pectore longa ferox', Ov. *Met.* 10. 402 'suspiria duxit ab imo / pectore'; ibid. 2. 753 'et tanto penitus traxit suspiria motu / ut pariter pectus positamque in pectore forti / aegida concuteret', Plaut. *Cist.* 55 'hoc sis vide, ut petivit / suspiritum alte'. For the absence of a preposition with *corde* cf. Hor. *Epod.* 11. 10 'latere petitus imo spiritus'. However, the missing word may have been something else, e.g. *quasso*; cf. Claud. *Rufin.* 1. 225 'effera praetumido quatiebat corda furore', Dracont. *Orest.* 119 'anxia sollicito quatiuntur corda pavore', Ov. *Met.* 2. 753 ff. (*supra*). Nor is *imo* (or *alto*) excluded; cf. 58 'quod temptabat opus. et amoris pluma tenebat', 125 'aut vox qualis erit? adgressum namque parentem'.

At sight of the girls who have been brought to distract him Perdica exclaims that, as he now sees, no other beauty can compare with his mother's. His love for her was, after all, inevitable. He continues with a rhetorical question (read *quid* for *sed* in 238): 'why do I try to conquer my passion by looking for allowable alternatives? 'hoc' (sc. *matris concubitum*) 'etiam voluisse nefas'. The sin has already been committed.

254   longaque testantur ieiunia viscera *fame*

fame *Hiller*: famem *H*

famem may have originally been a gloss on *ieiunia*. It is likely to have replaced *dura,* which fell out by haplography. In Silius' description of the famished Saguntines (2. 461) 'sedet acta (read *alta*; cf. 1. 59 'penitusque medullis / sanguinis humani flagrat sitis') medullis / iamdudum atque inopes penitus coquit intima pestis. / est furtim lento misere durantia tabo / viscera et exurit siccatas sanguine venas / per longum celata fames', *durantia* does not mean 'much-enduring'. Cf. Luc. 6. 93 'caeloque paratior unda / omne pati virus duravit viscera caeno', *et sim.*

275   ferro reseremus amorem?
        o demens! *gladio*? quibus armis quove vigore
        haec manus ecce valet librare in vulnera mortem?

gladio, imbecillic after *ferro,* is probably another piece of patchwork.
276 is likely to have started 'quid facis (*or* quid struis), o demens?', like Ov.
Met. 3. 641.

863a
<Iudicium Paridis>

2   hoc in discidio volumus, Paris, arbiter esto:
         cui pomum dederis, *titulum* simul ipse referto.

I make nothing of *titulum* or of Baehrens' comment 'an *ista,* ut *titulum*
valeat *gloriam*?' The goddesses were not about to offer Paris glory in return
for his verdict but other things. Venus begins in the next lines: 'plectra
sonora, ioci, lusus, lasciva voluptas, / haec mea. si reliquis me praefers,
ipsa puellam / pro mercede dabo, qua non formosior ulla'. Read *pretium.*